Research Within Reach II

Research Within Reach

II

Editors

Vicki Galloway
Georgia Institute of Technology

and

Carol Herron
Emory University

Southern Conference on Language Teaching
Valdosta State University
Valdosta, Georgia

© 1995
Southern Conference on Language Teaching
Valdosta State University
Valdosta, Georgia 31698

Library of Congress Catalogue Card Number: 94-61312
Printed in the United States of America
by Colson Printing Company
Valdosta, Georgia 31601

ISBN: 1-883640-03-2

Table of Contents

FOREWORD

The publication of this volume marks the passing of nearly a decade since the publication of the first volume of *Research Within Reach* by the Southern Conference on Language Teaching (SCOLT). The original 1985 publication arose from the efforts of a task force to provide convenient and easily accessible summaries of existing research in response to questions identified by classroom teachers. In their Foreword to the first volume of *Research Within Reach*, the authors describe their teacher-centered focus:

> ...we decided to adapt to our needs an approach for reporting research that has been successfully used by experts in the fields of communication, reading, and mathematics education...we decided first to discover from practitioners in the field what their most urgent questions were about foreign language learning and teaching. We then attempted to provide the answers by citing applicable research. Furthermore, we have tried to phrase our answers in straightforward language so readers would not be turned off by cumbersome, technical jargon.

It is this same field-driven approach that serves as the foundation of the present volume, *Research Within Reach II.*

Rationale for *Research Within Reach II*: A Closer Union

Leo Van Lier, in the following dialogue, captures what, for decades, has been perceived as the Great Divide:

> What is **theory**?
> --Practically irrelevant.
> What is **practice**?
> --Fine, in theory.

Education, in general, has not been characterized by a perfect collaboration between research and practice, perhaps because of the real-life factors that continuously wedge themselves between "**researchers**" and "**practitioners**": **time**, background, motivation, **time**, logistics, priorities, language, **time**. In addressing some of these factors in this volume of *Research Within Reach*, we have tried to provide an efficient vehicle for closing the distance between the researcher's "laboratory" and the teacher's classroom:

a) **Time**. Time is perhaps the principal enemy of the busy teacher who wishes to become more informed about research. For this reason, each topical chapter of *Research Within Reach II* presents a concise **synthesis** of available research in the areas targeted. These summaries not only provide an overview of some of the salient "findings" of research but, perhaps more importantly, serve also to expose some of the yet unanswered questions shared by researchers and practitioners alike. It should be noted, however, that summaries of research studies are, at best, a weak substitute for the real thing. Therefore, each chapter includes a lengthy bibliography which teachers are urged to consult for a more extensive and profound understanding of the issues addressed.

b) **Background and language**. Factors such as topical background and familiarity with terminology heavily influence the reader's access to a research study. If one is unaware of the issues, of previous research in the area, or of the meanings of certain terms used, understanding the report of a study can be quite a difficult undertaking. For this reason, a goal of the authors of *Research Within Reach II* has been to summarize the background issues and describe studies in comfortable, jargon-free language, to the greatest extent possible. Readers should bear in mind, however, that the use of some high-frequency terminology is not only unavoidable but, in fact, desirable, as it will likely be encountered throughout the research literature. Whenever they use a term is used that may be unfamiliar to readers, chapter authors have striven to explain or illustrate its use and meaning as clearly as possible.

c) **Priorities and Motivation**. A complaint teachers express frequently about research is that it is "too theoretical," "it doesn't have anything to do with my classroom," or "it doesn't address my needs as a teacher." For this reason, *Research Within Reach II* is constructed around concerns expressed by class-room teachers. Each chapter addresses an area of language teaching and learning and is structured around a series of specific questions culled from those submitted by classroom teachers. We hope and expect that you will find some of your questions among those that have been addressed and that, therefore, this volume will respond to your priorities as a foreign language teacher.

How to Use *Research Within Reach II*

While you may wish to begin reading *Research Within Reach II* by focusing on those chapters that address your most prominent concerns, it is hoped that you will eventually read the entire volume. There are many benefits to becoming informed of research in several areas, not the least of which is the recognition that studies overlap, draw from, and feed into other studies. Language learning and teaching are extremely complex undertakings that defy compartmentalization. Research in listening, for example, may both draw from and enrich research in reading, while holding implications for speaking and writing as well; technology-based research provides insights into learning processes and development of a number of skills; research in learner strategy use addresses issues in all areas of learning and interaction.

We highly recommended that you begin your travels through research by reading the short chapter that opens this volume, "Research Within the Teacher's Reach." In this chapter, Donna Johnson places the role and expectations of research in perspective in terms of what it can do and what it cannot do and provides succinct descriptions of both the purpose and limitations of certain types of studies. You may find especially valuable the step-by-step process Johnson provides teachers for conducting their own classroom-based research for, as you read the chapters of *Research Within Reach II* you will no doubt come up with many ideas and questions you will wish to explore. Indeed, research typically provides far more questions than answers.

Background of *Research Within Reach II*:
How Questions Were Generated

To help generate questions for authors to answer, members of the *Research Within Reach II* Advisory Committee asked foreign language teachers from their respective geographic regions to complete an exploratory questionnaire. It is important to emphasize that this questionnaire was distributed in an informal way; that is, no attempt was made to control the population for size, language(s) or level(s) taught, or for years of foreign language teaching experience.

In all, one hundred and forty-five teachers, primarily from elementary and secondary schools, agreed to complete the survey. The questionnaire had two primary sections. Teachers were asked:

1) to indicate the areas in which they would most like to have their teaching concerns and questions addressed;
2) to suggest four questions they would like to have answered about any aspect of foreign language learning and teaching.

Analysis of teachers' responses indicated that, indeed, teachers had many unanswered questions. Developing students' speaking proficiency was the area in which teachers expressed the highest concern in having their questions addressed. Perhaps this finding reflects the importance *students* place on developing speaking proficiency and teachers' perceived responsibility in helping them attain this goal. Listed in order of descending importance in terms of teachers' desire for information were the areas of learning processes and strategies, listening proficiency, testing learners' progress, integrating technology (tied in ranking with testing), teaching vocabulary, reading proficiency, teaching grammar, cultural proficiency, and writing proficiency. In reporting these findings, we stress that it is important to remember that respondents only indicated by their *rankings* those areas they most wanted to see discussed. The teachers were not asked to indicate the perceived importance of these areas in the teaching and learning of foreign languages.

As for the actual writing of questions, teachers submitted numerous questions in each of the previously mentioned areas. Unfortunately, we could not answer all of their worthwhile questions in the limited space of this volume. However, we feel strongly that the questions included in this volume are representative of what the teachers most often wanted to know. In many instances, the authors reformulated individual teacher questions (e.g., What are some IBM software titles for French and Spanish; or, How does one use the computer effectively in a large class?) into a more general research question (e.g., How can computers be used to improve conversation skills?). In this way, authors could address in their discussions as many of the teachers' queries as possible.

SCOLT Foreign Language Teacher Questionnaire

The Southern Conference on Language Teaching (SCOLT) seeks your assistance and expertise in a project to identify and address current questions and concerns of foreign language teachers. Please take a few minutes to reflect on the items below and provide us with your brief responses.

I. Background.

Language currently teaching: _____   Level(s)_____

Years of foreign language teaching experience: _____

II. Teaching/Learning Issues.

A. If you could have your teaching concerns and questions addressed in any of the following areas, which would you choose as having highest priority? Please rank the areas (or add your own) according to YOUR NEED for answers (#1 = highest concern).

___ **listening** proficiency   ___ teaching **vocabulary**

___ **reading** proficiency   ___ teaching **grammar**

___ **speaking** proficiency   ___ **testing** learners' progress

___ **writing** proficiency   ___ integrating **technology** (computers, video, etc.)

___ **cultural** proficiency   ___ learning **processes and strategies**

___ _____   ___ _____

B. List below **four questions** you would like to have answered about any aspect of foreign language **learning** and **teaching**. Please be as **specific** as possible (you may use the topics above as a guide, if you wish).

1.
2.
3.
4.

C. Please choose **one or more** of the areas listed in A above and, on the back of this sheet, briefly share your advice and expertise with other teachers. For each topic you selected, we would like you to tell us: 1) What, in your opinion, should all foreign language teachers know about this area? 2) How did **you** come to know this information?

THANK YOU!

ACKNOWLEDGMENTS

We would like to express our appreciation for the patience and support provided by the Southern Conference on Language Teaching (SCOLT) throughout the development of this volume, and particularly acknowledge the cooperation of Robert Terry, SCOLT Publications Chairman, and Lee Bradley, SCOLT Executive Director.
We extend our sincere gratitude also to the members of the *Research Within Reach II* Advisory Committee:

Lee Bradley	Valdosta State University
Ken Chastain	University of Virginia
Tom Cooper	University of Georgia
Greg Duncan	InterPrep, Atlanta
Olgalucía González	Washington and Jefferson College (WV)
Elizabeth Joiner	University of South Carolina
Robert Lafayette	Louisiana State University
Frank Medley	West Virginia University
Mimi Met	Montgomery (MD) County Schools
Genelle Morain	University of Georgia
James Noblitt	Institute for Academic Technology (NC)
Virginia Scott	Vanderbilt University
Robert Terry	University of Richmond

This hard-working committee helped us to conceptualize the project, design the survey instrument, collect and categorize data, and review manuscripts for each of the chapters. Their guidance and support were invaluable.
We also acknowledge with our thanks the teachers who submitted questions through our survey and the many anonymous reviewers who assisted us in reviewing the chapter manuscripts and in ensuring a format and style appropriate to our goals and our readership.
Finally, our special thanks go to the authors of the chapters of *Research Within Reach II*, who accepted the difficult task of responding to teachers' questions by not only synthesizing an enormous amount of research, but by presenting it with clear and accessible language. We much appreciated their patience and cooperative spirit.

Vicki Galloway and Carol Herron
Co-editors, *Research Within Reach II*

chapter 1

Research Within the Teacher's Reach

Donna M. Johnson
University of Arizona

QUESTION 1: **How can I become a better reader of research? How can I benefit more from the reports of research that I read? What should I look for when reading research reports?**

Discussion

I would like to introduce my answer to this question with some very general advice about reading research. I will then offer more specific suggestions for several different types of research. First, what should research do for teachers? Teachers can benefit more from research by developing a realistic set of expectations about what research **can** and **cannot** do. Some teachers sincerely expect research to provide definite answers about the best way to teach, or to prove that one method or technique is better than another. Yet, the idea that hard data can and should give us answers about what to do in the classroom is unrealistic and misguided. Research cannot be expected to provide prescriptive "shoulds" for teaching, and holding studies to such expectations can only lead to disappointment. Rather, it is much more productive to take the attitude that research can enrich our understanding of the complexities of language learning and teaching and can serve as one source of new ideas.

Second, what should teachers do with research findings? Teachers can become better readers of research by abandoning a mechanical, "consumer model" of applying research. This traditional model assumes that researchers conduct research, and that the role of the teacher is simply that of receiving and applying these findings to the classroom. Yet teachers, as readers of research, are not simply passive recipients of information. Rather, teachers (like all readers) are active constructors of meaning. That is, they must always make judgments about the ways in which a particular study may or may not apply to a different set of learners, in a different teaching situation, and in a different cultural setting. They then must create applications for their own situations. Applying research is not a mechanical process, but involves creative thinking based on new insights.

What to look for when reading research depends on the type of study you are reading. In studies that are **quantitative** in orientation—such as experiments, surveys, and correlational studies—you can expect to find results reported primarily in the form of numbers. You can also expect to find careful discussion of the procedures that were followed in carrying out the study. In research that is **qualitative** in orientation—such as ethnographic research and case studies—you can expect to find fewer numbers and more emphasis on rich descriptions of students, teachers, classrooms, and the learning contexts. In research involving **discourse analysis** (the study of language use beyond the sentence level), you can expect to find detailed descriptions of the language used, such as students' written or oral production, the language used in classroom interaction, or the language of textbooks. I will provide several suggestions about what to look for in reading research of each of these types.

In *correlational studies*, researchers either gather information in quantitative form (in the form of numbers) or they convert the information gathered to a numerical form. They do this because numbers are needed to conduct the statistical analyses. Consequently, the value of a correlational study rests heavily on how well the *constructs* are defined and measured. Examples of *constructs* are language proficiency, cultural attitudes, and anxiety. In reading a study, then, it is important to decide for yourself how well the constructs are defined and measured. To do this, examine the instruments that were used in the study. For example, if a questionnaire was given to students, read the actual questionnaire items (you can usually find the questionnaire in the appendix). As you read the items, think about how the participants or "subjects" in the study might have responded. How well do the items assess what they were intended to assess? How might the students have responded differently under different circumstances? Are you convinced that these items provide credible measures? Your answers to these questions will help you decide how to interpret the results.

A second issue to think about in reading correlational studies is that of **causality**. In a study that demonstrates a positive relationship between attitudes and language proficiency, for example, we do not know whether positive attitudes were the **cause** of higher proficiency or whether higher proficiency was the cause of positive attitudes. It might be that each continually interacts with and influences the other.

Even though the directions of causality may be impossible to determine, good correlational studies can make us aware of the many factors involved in language learning and open our eyes to new associations among them.

Surveys, like correlational studies, are quite common in our field and can provide us with valuable information about current trends in language teaching. The goal of a *survey* is to provide information about a population (an entire group of interest) by studying a sample (a subset of that group). In reading reports of survey research, as in reading correlational studies, it is important to look for and examine the actual instruments (such as questionnaires) that were used to gather information. Try to determine how well the questions get at the important issues.

A second important consideration in survey research is potential nonresponse bias due to low response rates. Look for the response rate. What percentage of the sample actually responded to the questionnaire? A response rate of 90% is considered high; rates in the 70s and 80s are more common; rates in the 60s or below are usually too low. When response rates are low, the results may be biased. That is, those persons who did not respond might have provided very different answers from those who did respond. While there are many other important considerations in reading survey research, examining the actual instruments and evaluating the response rates are important steps that will help you decide how to interpret the results.

Experiments, unlike surveys, involve the study of **planned change**. The experimenter designs the treatments or tasks, sets them up, and examines their effects. While there are many kinds of experiments, experimental research might involve, for example, comparing three different ways of presenting a grammar-focused lesson to determine which best promotes learning. Or an experimenter might compare different ways of structuring tasks for communicative practice to see which way will result in higher quality language use. Suppose, for example, that you are reading a report of an experiment that compares two different ways of structuring a task to determine which one results in richer language use by small groups of students. One of the most important things to look for in reading such a study is a description of the tasks and how they were structured. The researcher should clearly explain the ways in which task A was similar to and different from task B.

You should also try to determine whether the results are actually attributable to the differences in task structure. Because experiments are designed to establish a cause-and-effect relationship, you need to consider for yourself whether the differences in the results for the two groups are attributable to the treatments or to some other causes. What other factors might have influenced the results? Look for information about the teachers, students, classrooms, or wider contexts that might help explain the results.

Third, look for ways to generalize the findings of the experiment. While the researcher will usually provide some discussion of the generalizability of the results, both researchers and readers of research often overgeneralize. You should be careful not to make inappropriate generalizations to other persons, other cultural groups, other age groups, other settings, or other task conditions. On the other hand, even though the students in the study might have been very different from your own students, that is no reason to dismiss the entire study as irrelevant. Instead, look for ways to use **insights** from the research. For example, the study might help you understand what to expect from students, or it might give you ideas for tasks, assignments, or assessment.

Experiments, correlational studies, and surveys usually provide information about groups of students. Case studies, on the other hand, usually provide detailed descriptions of one or a few students. A *case study* is a disciplined examination of one or more cases in context. A case can be a student, but it might also be a teacher, class, or other entity. Sometimes researchers study several cases and compare them. For example, one researcher studied and compared the learning strategies of three different students in a high-school French class: one who was becoming trilingual in Spanish, English and French; another in Navajo, English, and French; and the third in Russian, English and French.

An important consideration in case-study research is thoroughness. Look for evidence that the researcher spent enough time studying the students, teachers, or classrooms as well as the relevant contexts to fully understand the issues. Along these same lines, look for evidence of **triangulation**—evidence that the researcher gathered information from various sources and in various ways to answer the research questions adequately. Such thoroughness helps avoid descriptions that are based only on initial impressions.

Teachers with strong interests in cultural phenomena as they relate to language use, language learning, and teaching may want to read *ethnographic research*. The purpose of ethnographic research is to describe and interpret the cultural behavior, including communicative behavior, of a group. In reading ethnographic accounts, look for rich or "thick" descriptions of the cultural setting—descriptions that involve *cultural interpretation*; that is, look for interpretations of the meaning that particular social actions and events have for the participants from their own cultural perspective. You might also find it interesting to look for the author's definition of culture. The knowledge gained from ethnographic research not only helps teachers better understand their students' attitudes, values, and behavior, but can also serve as a source of ideas about teaching language and culture in an integrated manner.

An important characteristic of ethnographic research is that, unlike experimental research, in which researchers manipulate conditions, ethnographic research involves studying phenomena in their natural state and as unobtrusively as possible.

Data collection involves a great deal of watching and asking. In reading ethnographic accounts, then, look for evidence of **long-term** observation and much interviewing. You can also expect to find discussion of the roles the researcher played throughout the study.

A final approach to research that has become very prominent in L2 studies is *discourse analysis*, the study of language use beyond the sentence level. All teachers analyze their students' discourse continually as they read and comment on compositions, for example, as they help students construct role plays, or as they assess a story-retelling task. Moreover, all teachers also analyze their own oral discourse (or "teacher talk") as they reflect on their teaching style and make decisions about how to make their own language comprehensible to students or how to encourage fluency or accuracy during conversational practice in the classroom. More formal forms of discourse analysis are widely used within each of the types of research described above. When reading studies involving discourse analysis, look for clear definitions and examples of the terms or categories used in the analysis. Once you understand the terms the author is using, you will probably be able to understand the study. There is no substitute for taking courses or studying to gain a fuller understanding of research methodology (see, for example, Johnson, 1992). But even without a high level of knowledge about statistics or ethnography, for example, much can be learned from reading research. Just as we encourage language learners to be risk-takers and to tolerate partial knowledge of the L2, we, ourselves, while always continuing to learn, must tolerate incomplete knowledge of research methods and theories. One of the best ways to learn about research is through hands-on experience. Many teachers find that conducting their own pilot research projects is an exciting and "eye-opening" experience.

QUESTION 2: If I have a question about teaching and learning that really interests me, how can I go about finding answers? How can I get started with a teacher research project?

Discussion

First, you will need to make a time commitment. Because research is **disciplined inquiry**, doing classroom research requires stepping aside from normal teaching activities and taking the time to look closely and extensively at an issue that you want to know more about. It takes time to plan the study, to collect information, to analyze the information, to refocus the study as needed, to collect additional information, to analyze it, to collaborate with colleagues, and to share your plans and findings at various stages of the project. Because of the time, discipline, and expertise required to conduct research, a good way to get started is to do a pilot study. Some teachers study their own classrooms, while some work in others' classrooms.

In this section, I propose a general plan for getting started in conducting a teacher-research project. I have used this approach for several years in graduate courses with experienced teachers. The major goals of a pilot research project are to ask an important and interesting question, to seek answers to the question, and to seek explanations for the answers. It is best to begin with a small pilot study rather than attempting to gather information from a large number of students or classes. With a small study, one can focus on rich description and explanation. A useful approach, therefore, is to conduct an essentially qualitative or descriptive study, perhaps a case study, that may involve some quantification in various phases of analysis.

Developing a topic. Over a period of several weeks, make a list of 20 broad questions that interest you. Write these in the form of questions that would require an extensive answer. Then, carefully review your list. Which themes are salient, recurring, and most compelling? Select a theme and write one broad research question. It is more productive to write How and Why questions rather than yes/no questions or questions that begin with "What is the best way to . . . ?" How and why questions lead to richer descriptions and better attempts at explanation which, in turn, are more useful for gaining a deeper understanding of teaching and learning processes. For example, the initial driving question for two teachers (a teacher of German and an ESOL teacher of adults) was "What is the best way to get students to use more of the target language in group work?" The ESOL teacher reformulated this question as: "For what purposes do students chose to use each language in group work?" When she gained a richer understanding of students' reasons for selecting one language or the other, she was then better prepared to make informed decisions about altering her classroom practices. The German teacher reformulated the question as: "How is language choice related to task type and group composition?" Her answers to this question provided her with solid information on which to base changes in group activities.

Let's consider another example of how to reformulate a question. The initial question of a teacher and her two research partners was: "What is the best way to teach vocabulary?" They reformulated this question as: "What strategies do three students of different language and cultural backgrounds bring to the task of acquiring, recycling, and retaining new vocabulary?" Examples of other initial research questions from my graduate students, all experienced teachers, include: (1) How is the video-based foreign language program functioning in elementary-school classrooms and what roles are the grade-level teachers playing? (2) What are teacher and student attitudes and practices regarding error correction? (3) What are some sources of comprehension problems for two Mexican graduate students studying plant sciences and how do they cope? (4) What are the differences between male and female discourse in pair activities in a second-year foreign language classroom?

Once you have constructed a broad research question, start writing. Writing is an excellent way to reflect—to discover what you are thinking and to encourage further thinking. Write down your observations and ideas about the topic and save them for comparison with your later work. First, why are you interested in the issue? What have you noticed and how have your observations affected your thinking? What are your beliefs, biases, and personal theories about this issue? For example, in describing his beliefs, one of my graduate students, an experienced teacher from China, wrote, "Personally, I believe that all the errors made by students should be corrected one way or another . . . To me, ignoring errors is like abandoning teaching." Another teacher wrote that she expected the Japanese student in her study to be conscientious but quiet in class, while she expected the Spanish speaker to rely on social strategies for language learning. To her surprise, her predictions were wrong. All teachers act on the basis of beliefs or personal theories about how students learn and how teaching practices "work." Therefore, it is an eye-opening experience to state your personal theories explicitly and then reexamine them in light of what you learn in your study. To document these changes, it is important to write during every phase of the project.

Gathering information and writing: Phase 1. Once you have established a broad question and written on the topic, make plans to conduct at least two observations and two interviews to explore the topic and seek initial answers to your question. Depending on your question, you might observe two classrooms and interview the two teachers, or you might observe and interview two students. It is important to keep the focus broad at this point, because your goal is to gain a broad understanding of the issue in context. Take detailed notes and record as much potentially relevant contextual information as possible. Contextual information might include classroom procedures, the school context, teachers' roles, student characteristics, cultural issues, or students' home life.

Within one day of conducting an observation or interview, write a detailed account of what you learned. In this way, details can be filled in before they are forgotten. Write your findings in narrative/qualitative form. What are some tentative or potential answers to your broad research question? Include a full description of the contextual factors that you learned about and try to explain, or at least speculate about, how these contextual factors relate to and help explain the issue under study. In what ways did what you learned differ from your expectations? What surprises did you encounter? For example, one teacher and her research partner set out to examine an aspect of student language use (discourse) in small-group activities. They were surprised to find that the males "completely dominated interactions" during group work. This initial finding was so striking that they refocused their study to systematically examine gender differences in interaction. After gathering information and writing during Phase 1, share your initial observations and interpretations with others and record (write down) their questions and ideas.

Gathering information and writing: Phase 2. Next, formulate questions for a second phase of information gathering and writing. Based on what you learned from Phase 1, your reading, and your thinking, what are some of the more specific questions that you hope to answer in Phase 2 of data collection? Write about three specific research questions (in the form of questions). These questions should relate directly to the broad question and reflect a tightening up of your research objectives. They should be What, How, or Why questions rather than yes/no questions.

Then make plans for your second phase of data collection. Decide how you can best collect the information that will help you answer these questions. As in Phase 1, this involves field work—gathering empirical information. You might conduct more observations; conduct additional interviews with students or teachers; video-tape and begin to analyze activities, lessons, conversations, interviews; gather and begin to analyze student written work; or combine several data-collection techniques. Before collecting data, write out what you expect to find in Phase 2. What are your biases, beliefs, personal theories at this point? Make these explicit.

Collect data according to your plan. Immediately after collecting data, write up your findings. Describe your roles—what you did, where, with whom, how, and for how long. Then, describe in detailed, narrative format, what you learned. [For a good guide to writing up qualitative research, see Wolcott, 1990.] How does what you learned help answer both the broad question and the specific questions? In what ways did what you learned differ from your expectations? Why? What were some of the important contextual factors, and how do these contextual factors help explain the phenomena that you are investigating? After two phases of data collection, analysis, and writing, you should be ready to develop a more formal research design. A *research design* is a plan that specifies in detail what procedures you will use to carry out the study. At this point, you need to plan carefully for additional data collection and additional analysis.

Reading the literature. Even though you may have conducted a thorough review of the recent and relevant research literature in planning your project, it is important to continue reading throughout the project. Your reading will help you discover new ways of looking at phenomena and help you develop new conceptual categories and the vocabulary for discussing them (see, for example, Omaggio Hadley, 1993). Conversely, what you are learning in the field will lead your reading in additional directions and will increase your understanding of the literature. As one teacher wrote, "My own case-study research not only clarified for me the best routes to take in helping both of the students, but it also helped me to make sense of all the rest of the research on the topic." You may also decide to read research in related fields such as cognitive psychology, anthropology, or sociolinguistics to expand your knowledge and lead your thinking in additional directions.

Analyzing the data. Careful and thorough data analysis is crucial throughout the project. Initial analyses conducted after Phases 1 and 2 need to be supplemented by thorough analysis of additional data. The type of analysis will depend entirely on the research questions you pose and the data you collect. For pilot projects that are case studies, an approach that is often feasible is to combine primarily qualitative analysis with some quantification that will serve to indicate how frequently certain phenomena occur. In a general sense, you will need to (1) search repeatedly through your data for meaningful patterns and information that help answer your questions, and then (2) search again for explanations for those answers. If you decide to analyze the written or spoken language of students, Hatch's (1992) book on discourse analysis provides many practical ideas. Regardless of the methods of analysis selected, research is not disciplined inquiry without analysis. It is at the careful analysis phase that many pilot research projects fall apart.

Sharing your insights. Select a way to share your research with others: a story, a workshop for colleagues, a conference presentation, a newsletter or journal article, a proposal for funding, a plan for an experimental class or program. In your account, make connections between the research and theory that you have read, what you learned in the field, and how you modified your personal theories and attitudes about learning and teaching. Then, make specific suggestions for teaching and invite your audience to create suggestions that might make sense for different kinds of classrooms. As Lightbown (1994) points out, teachers and researchers have different responsibilities, but both have an interest in improving classroom language teaching. There is no doubt that your research project will benefit you and your own students, but it can be very rewarding if you share your insights and contribute even in some small way to improving teaching for others as well.

Bibliography

Hatch, E. 1992. *Discourse and Language Education*. Cambridge: Cambridge University Press.

Johnson, D. M. 1992. *Approaches to Research in Second Language Learning*. White Plains, NY: Longman.

Lightbown, P. M. 1994. *Teachers and Researchers: Both Oars in the Water*. Plenary address at the annual meeting of the American Association for Applied Linguistics, Baltimore, MD.

Omaggio Hadley, A., ed. 1993. *Research in Language Learning: Principles, Processes, and Prospects*. Lincolnwood, IL: National Textbook.

Wolcott, H. F. 1990. *Writing Up Qualitative Research*. Newbury Park, CA: Sage.

Publisher's Note

An excellent glossary of terms used in research is found on pages 279-94 of the Omaggio Hadley (1993) book listed above.

chapter 2

Learning Processes and Learner Strategies

Joan Rubin
Independent Consultant

QUESTION 1: How do students learn? What are the similarities and differences between L1 and L2 acquisition? What is the relation of teaching to learning?

Discussion

These are extremely important and complex questions. Probably the most critical change in the recent research literature is the notion of the learner as an **active processor** of information. One metaphor for this view of learning is to think of language learners as scientists; as information comes in, they compare it to the information they already have, then make and test hypotheses about how the new language works.

This kind of processing appears to involve a great deal of trial and error-learners can be expected to make mistakes as they work toward understanding the many details of a language. In earlier times, when learning was often considered to be the result of habit formation, teachers were enjoined to make sure that student errors were corrected immediately or, it was assumed, the errors would never go away. Now, research suggests that learning is a process of "successive approximation;" this is, learners try out their own hypotheses and observe how they work. The resulting learner language is sometimes called an "interlanguage," as it reflects the interim hypotheses of the learner. Many researchers argue that this type of cognitive processing takes place in both L1 and L2 learning. For example, a very young child acquiring English as L1 may, at an early stage in acquisition, be heard uttering such forms as "he goed," forms which the child has never heard an adult use. Such an utterance reflects the hypothesis that the past tense is formed by adding the suffix "**-ed**". At a later date, however, the child notes that "**went**" is somehow an exception to this hypothesis and, therefore, adds it to a growing linguistic repertoire.

In order to form hypotheses, both L1 and L2 learners need a **context** in which to interpret what is going on and, thus, formulate meaning. Their interpretations are based on clues and knowledge they already have about the language, the world, and human relationships. The more the context relates directly to what is being said, the easier becomes the task of understanding. Obviously, learners with more experience and more knowledge may need fewer clues and may be able to arrive at better hypotheses more efficiently. Hypothesis formation, then, is facilitated by the richness of context and background knowledge. Advocates of using video as a learning tool in the language classroom argue for its power to facilitate hypothesis formation by linking language to other kinds of information: physical setting, action, gestures, emotions, or knowledge about the world.

Another similarity between L1 and L2 learners is that both appear to need a lot of auditory input before they can produce oral language. In other words, learners need extensive and intensive opportunities to listen to a foreign language so they can become accustomed to how it sounds and so they can formulate hypotheses about the system (Postovsky, 1974). [For discussion of comprehension-based models of language learning, see Shrum and Glisan, 1994.]

There are, of course, some major differences between L1 and L2 learning. First, L2 learners have already learned a first language, so they already have some idea about how a language works and, therefore, a basis for comparison. Secondly, they have a great deal of background knowledge that L1 learners do not have about the world, about interpersonal relations, and about the kinds of dramas that occur. This knowledge appears to assist them in formulating and testing their hypotheses. Third, if L2 learning takes place after puberty, learners usually have developed stronger analytical and pattern-finding skills to assist them in forming and testing hypotheses. Also, they have developed a sense of logical thinking, which allows them to better analyze how a language works. Finally, some researchers suggest that, as children grow, two kinds of knowledge develop: **declarative knowledge** (what they know) and **procedural knowledge** (how they go about learning) (Anderson, 1983; O'Malley et al., 1987). **Declarative knowledge** includes such things as knowing vocabulary or grammar, or knowing how to conduct a conversation or write an essay. **Procedural knowledge** includes knowing **how to learn** a language-an awareness of efficient strategies for organizing and remembering information, or the ability to recognize the difficulty of a task and plan one's study accordingly. Second language learners can be more effective in learning the L2 because they have these two sources of knowledge to draw upon to facilitate the process.

What might these differences between L1 and L2 learning mean for the teaching-learning process? First, they suggest that teachers begin to see themselves as **collaborators** with learners, guiding learners in the **process** of acquiring the language as well as providing information about the language. Second, an important role of the teacher will be to provide what has been called a "haven for learning" (Bransford, et al., 1985), in which students are active and constant participants. This will mean constructing opportunities and providing guidance to learners in connecting experiences and in using available information to make sense. The teacher's role, however, is not only to facilitate the learning process but also to foster learner autonomy by helping students improve their **procedural knowledge** of how language learning occurs.

QUESTION 2: How can I help my students become more aware of and responsible for their own learning?

Discussion

There are many things a teacher can do to help students become more responsible for their own language learning. The first step is to help learners become aware of **what they do to learn**, to help them assess their own approaches to learning tasks. This assessment can be done in several ways: (1) Sometimes, it helps for learners to fill out an overall survey of how they approach learning. Several types of questionnaires are available to help learners assess their approach to learning (O'Malley and Chamot, 1990; Oxford, 1990; Wenden, 1991; Rubin and Thompson, 1994). (2) Many students find it helpful to keep a regular diary of their learning, which the teacher can review on a regular basis. The diary should probably be written in the student's L1 so that it can be done more easily and in greater depth. (3) During a class, teachers can ask more successful learners how they arrived at a particular answer. Often, the response comes as a surprise to less expert learners. The less competent learner may begin to feel the task is not so onerous and decide, "Oh, I can do that too." (4) Students may find it useful to read about the topic of learner strategies and the importance of being engaged while learning (Rubin and Thompson, 1994). (5) Teachers can facilitate regular discussions about student problems in each of the skill areas and about how students can and do handle the problem themselves.

Another thing that teachers can do is to involve students in setting objectives. It is helpful for students to work at stating their goals clearly and establishing a realistic time frame in which the goals will be accomplished. Students who tend to think of their goals in overly broad terms, such as "to speak the language," or "to carry on a conversation," may be guided to set clear, functional objectives and progress markers, the achievement of which they, themselves can monitor: "to ask the time" or "to order a meal," for example. With specified, realistic, use-oriented goals, learners can judge for themselves what they are able to do and what they are not able to do yet and, therefore, can have more control of, and take more responsibility for their learning. Instead of unilateral, teacher-set goals, the purpose of which learners may not even understand, goals should be ones that learners have articulated or worked out with the teacher.

Finally, teachers can help students consider the role of their language learning beliefs (Horwitz, 1987; Wenden, 1991). Research has shown that students are more likely to succeed when they 1) have a clear understanding of how language learning works, and 2) place responsibility for learning largely on themselves. There appears to be a dynamic interplay between students' motivation and beliefs and their ability to use their higher thinking skills.

Expert learners not only are aware of their beliefs and their strategies, they are in control of their learning. Research has shown that effective learners have an arsenal of **cognitive strategies** they use to learn a language (such as good ways to use their background knowledge to learn new information), which they combine effectively with **metacognitive strategies** (ways of thinking **about** the learning process) to plan, monitor, and evaluate their learning. Planning involves goal definition (for example, "to learn how to introduce myself") and an action plan ("within one week—learn the rules, practice to myself, practice with peers or native speakers"). Monitoring involves noting whether what one has planned is working, noting sources of difficulty (problematic portions), and noting successes. Evaluating means determining whether to revise one's plans or language use in some way. The learner who plans, monitors, and evaluates is using "executive control." Research has shown that expert learners have well developed executive control [See: Wenden, 1982; Brown and Baker, 1984; Wenden and Rubin, 1987; O'Malley and Chamot, 1990].

Teachers can help develop monitoring in a number of ways:

✎ **Teachers can set up exercises to help students see their own errors.** For example, Henner-Stanchina (1985) has created a listening exercise to encourage learners to notice that meaning often derives from relationships between sentences. In this exercise, learners take a dictation on a four-sentence dialogue and are then asked to review their dictation to be sure it makes sense. This process causes them to monitor their performance beyond the individual sentence and to improve their listening comprehension on their own.

✦ **Teachers can help learners make choices about strategy use.** A video experiment by Thompson and Rubin (1993), for example, provided three genres of video texts: interview, news, and drama. After watching each genre with the sound off, students came to the conclusion that this strategy was most helpful with drama and somewhat helpful with some interviews, but that the visual provided little help in understanding the news. While watching the news broadcast, learners came to the conclusion that, after one viewing with both audio and video on, it was helpful to turn the video off because it was too distracting. Learners also recognized that certain strategies worked best with specific genres (for example, recognizing and looking for the question-and-answer format in interviews).

✦ **Teachers can encourage students to be more specific about what they don't understand and to ask the teacher or others for clarification on a regular basis.**

✦ **Teachers can suggest alternative strategies for learners to use.** Research shows that while all learners use cognitive strategies, good learners **examine** their use of strategies and change them as needed. If students have an arsenal of strategies and begin to evaluate their use of these strategies, they will begin to take control of their learning. Learners need to become aware of their responsibility to determine (1) what it is they don't understand-linguistic or sociolinguistic aspects; (2) whether that lack of knowledge is critical to the total communication; and (3) whether their choice of strategies is facilitating their learning.

QUESTION 3: What strategies do successful learners use?

Discussion

Both expert and novice learners use the same set of learning strategies. However, research shows that expert learners use these strategies more effectively, varying their use of strategies according to the task, according to their proficiency level, and according to the language skill being practiced. For example, when the task is writing, expert learners recognize that accuracy is called for, whereas it may not be so critical in some types of speaking tasks. Some research shows that expert learners also use strategies more frequently. However, all current research agrees that whatever strategies students use, it is important that they have an awareness of this usage and are able to self-assess their strategy use so as to change course as needed.

The following is just one of the several typologies researchers have developed to describe the cognitive strategies used by expert learners (Rubin, 1987; O'Malley and Chamot, 1990; Oxford, 1990).

    ✦ **Clarification or verification.** This category refers to those strategies which learners use to verify or clarify their understanding of the new language. Asking how to pronounce a word or asking if one can use a word in a new context are examples of this type of strategy. Teachers can facilitate use of this strategy by teaching students how to ask for clarification in L2.

    ✦ **Guessing/inductive inferencing.** This category of strategies refers to such tactics as the use of background knowledge (linguistic, cultural, world, textual) to derive explicit hypotheses about form, meaning, or expression of intention. For example, using visual information and world knowledge to infer the storyline; using world knowledge to order in a restaurant; using the genre type to predict content; or using cognates to guess the meaning of new words. Teachers can facilitate use of this strategy by (a) showing video without sound to encourage attention to visuals; (b) asking students to brainstorm about the kind of questions and answers one would expect in a waiter-customer exchange, then verifying predictions by viewing a video segment; (c) asking students to consider what kind of information might be found in a newscast, a narrative, or an ad; (d) asking students to identify and guess the meanings of cognates they encounter.

    ✦ **Deductive reasoning.** This category of strategies refers to the search for and use of general rules to derive specific hypotheses about form or meaning. For example, students may use analogy to determine meaning or analyze several forms to deduce a general rule. Teachers can promote use of deduction by providing an array of ways of organizing information and asking learners to consider the relationships between these different ways. There are many ways to organize grammatical and lexical information; students should be helped to find those ways that work best for them.

⟡   **Practice.** This category refers to strategies that contribute to the storage and retrieval of language and focus on the **accuracy of usage.** Examples include rehearsal of information, experimentation, imitation. Teachers can promote use of practice by providing opportunities to experiment in class or by encouraging students to try out new vocabulary by creating stories about the topic of a lesson.

⟡   **Memorization.** This category refers to strategies that focus on the **storage and retrieval** of language. The goal of these strategies is organization. Examples include finding some sort of association or grouping (phonetic, semantic, visual, auditory, kinesic, even olfactory or sensory); using one word to recall a number of others (called key word); using some sort of mechanical means to store information; focusing on certain details to aid in recall; and associating language items or features with physical movement. Teachers can facilitate memory by having students first brainstorm about their own memory techniques and then practice using some new ones to determine which ones work best for them. [For techniques for teaching memory strategies, see Cohen, 1990; Oxford, 1990.]

QUESTION 4: How do I teach strategies?

Discussion

Teaching good strategy use takes time. Adding to and improving a learner's procedural knowledge is as important and as complex a procedure as adding to a learner's declarative knowledge about the language. Since learner strategy instruction is so important and takes so long, teachers should plan to incorporate the teaching of learner strategies in the regular curriculum.

There are three ways to teach strategies: **blind, informed,** and **control. Blind** strategy instruction involves providing an exercise that requires use of strategies (such as a cloze test which relies on surrounding context), but in which neither the text nor the teacher states what strategy is being used or why. **Informed** strategy instruction requires that the teacher label the strategy as it is being taught and tell students why it is useful. **Controlled** strategy instruction involves not only labeling a strategy and telling why it is useful, but also offering opportunities for learners to select which strategy they will use and to explain why they chose it. In other words, with this latter kind of strategy instruction, learners are helped in the development of their executive control. Research has shown that while all three kinds of strategy instruction improve student performance, informed strategy instruction yields better results than blind instruction and controlled strategy instruction yields the best results, regardless of the task (Brown and Palincsar, 1982).

Students will vary in how much strategy instruction they need. Expert learners (that 2-5% of the class who are outstanding without much assistance) can be helped to sharpen their strategies but may need little instruction. However, the majority of students will need quite a bit of strategy instruction. One way to keep expert learners involved in strategy instruction is to ask them to state aloud how they executed a particular task, or what they did to remember, or how they understood a video passage. Students will not only feel good about their own strategies, but will also provide valuable insights for more novice learners.

Learner strategy instruction involves continual assessment of strategy use (either by a questionnaire, diary, or class discussion) and awareness of an array of strategies. Eventually, students will integrate strategy use into their procedural knowledge and develop automaticity. At every stage of learning, students will encounter a new set of problems and may need to adjust their strategy use or consider using other strategies.

Currently, there are a number of useful texts to learn about types of strategies and how to teach them. Wenden (1991) is a fine introduction to learner autonomy. Oxford (1990) offers an extensive set of classroom exercises to introduce learning strategies. Willing (1991) provides a number of activities to use in ESL classes which can easily be adapted to foreign language classes.

QUESTION 5: What is the role of memory in learning? What kinds of activities can improve memory?

Discussion

Learning involves getting, storing, retrieving and using information. Memory is a critical part of learning, since it is involved in the getting and storing of information as well as the ability to retrieve that information. The view of a learner as an **active processor** has important implications for memory. Teachers need to consider what will help the learner process information.

First, memory appears to work best by **association**, since this strategy allows the learner to make linkages among the words to be learned. If learners can connect new information to old information, the process of storage is facilitated. The more mental networks and connections are formed, the more retrieval of information is facilitated.

Second, sensory or emotional associations appear to facilitate storage and retrieval. One reason why advocates of Total Physical Response (Asher, 1982) find it an effective technique is that students associate the new language input not only with auditory and visual input, but also with kinesthetic input. Research also indicates that the more connections with **different** senses, the more effective are storage and retrieval. There is quite a body of information supporting the conclusion that information is usually stored with **affective coding**. In other words, if something is important enough to the learner to cause some emotion, there is a higher likelihood that it will be stored more efficiently and retrieved quite readily. [See Hatch and Yoshitomi, 1993, for a discussion of memory and L2.]

Finally, memory varies from person to person and from skill to skill. Some people have quite expert memories without any training. However, research shows that memory can be improved with training. [See Cohen and Aphek, 1980, for a discussion of L2 memory training.] It is clear that memory plays a critical role in listening comprehension because of the requirement for on-line processing. When learners have a low level of proficiency (few language networks or associations), they can concentrate only on very small amounts of language at a time. As their knowledge of the language builds, they are able to listen to and store larger amounts of language.

Although rote learning is largely considered the least efficient memory strategy, there is one situation in which rote learning can be quite helpful. Novice learners should be encouraged to memorize a few formulaic utterances to help them remain in a conversation so they can continue to get input and improve their hypothesis-building (Wong-Fillmore, 1976).

QUESTION 6: How does one both motivate students and put them at ease in the language learning environment?

Discussion

Motivation appears to have three general components: (1) students' beliefs about the importance and value of the task (**value components**), (2) students' beliefs about their ability or skill to perform the task (**expectancy components**), and (3) students' feelings about themselves or their emotional reactions to the task (**affective components**) (Pintrich, 1989).

A teacher can address each of these components and help enhance student motivation. With regard to the value component, students need to have tasks that are **meaningful** to them. Assigning meaningful tasks assumes several things:

- ⬧ Classroom communication should relate to a real need to get information, not just provide mechanical practice

- ⬧ Learners need to have **choices** among tasks so that they can select those that are of greatest interest to them

- ⬧ Students should be involved in setting goals so that goals are clear, meaningful, and important.

The expectancy component is especially critical. The best ways to help learners improve their beliefs about themselves are: (1) to provide instruction in learner strategies so that students build their confidence and (2) to organize materials so that learners experience immediate success and increased confidence in their ability. In a recent experiment with high school students of Spanish (Rubin, 1990), learners were taught about cognates before being exposed to a listening-comprehension task. Learners were asked to identify cognates in a video passage. They were then asked to tell the story of the video. The lesson provided learner strategy instruction and used materials that included a number of cognates to be discovered. The results of this activity were quite motivating. In fact, one student exclaimed: "I like this exercise. It makes me feel smart." When learner ability improves, learner expectancy improves, and, in turn, improves affect (Pintrich, 1989).

With regard to the affective components, researchers have found that it is important to help learners come to grips with their feelings about learning a language. Learners need to develop strategies to recognize and come to terms with their frustrations, their fears, their concerns. Learning a new language is a complex and demanding task. It is important that learners recognize that while learning a language they may have some strong feelings which may need to be addressed in order for them to be more effective in achieving their language goals.

Students also need to learn ways to lower their anxiety, to encourage themselves, and to continually take their emotional temperature (Oxford, 1990). For example, they can engage in positive self-talk, they can write a language learning diary or journal to keep track of events and feelings while learning a language, or they can talk with another person to exchange feelings about learning a language.

By providing instruction in cognitive and metacognitive strategies, by providing instruction in affective strategies, by involving the learner in selecting goals, by improving the learner's self-concept, teachers can go a long way toward putting students at ease. Learners will also be more comfortable with the learning process when teachers view language learning as a process of successive approximation and approach errors in a constructive manner. Finally, as all teachers know, introducing humor and play into the class will contribute a great deal to lowering learner anxiety.

Bibliography

Anderson, J. R. 1983. *The Architecture of Cognition*. Cambridge, MA: Harvard University Press.

Asher, J. J. 1982. *Learning Another Language Through Actions: The Complete Teacher's Guidebook*. 2nd ed. Los Gatos, CA: Sky Oaks Productions.

Bransford, J. D., R. D. Sherwood, C. K. Kinzer, and T. S. Hasselbring. 1985. *Havens for Learning: Toward a Framework for Developing Effective Uses of Technology*. Nashville: George Peabody College for Teachers.

Brown, A. L. and A. S. Palncsar. 1982. "Inducing Learning from Texts by Means of Informed Self-Control Training," *Topics in Learning and Learning Disabilities* 2, 1-17. [Special Issue on Metacognition and Learning Disabilities]

Brown, A. and L. Baker. 1984. "Metacognitive Skills and Reading," in P.O. Pearson, ed., *Handbook of Reading Research*. New York: Longman.

Cohen, A. 1990. *Language Learning*. New York: Newbury House.

Cohen, A. and E. Aphek. 1980. "Retention of Second-Language Vocabulary Over Time: Investigating the Role of Mnemonic Associations." *System* 8,3: 221-35.

Hatch, E. and A. Yoshitomi. 1993. "Cognitive Processes in Language Learning," in A. Omaggio Hadley, ed., *Research in Language Learning*. Lincolnwood, IL: National Textbook

Henner-Stanchina, C. 1985. "Metacognitive Awareness Training for Listening Comprehension: Integrating A Metacognitive Awareness Training Component into a Listening Comprehension Course." Unpublished paper.

Horwitz, E. K. 1987. "Surveying Student Beliefs about Language Learning," in A. Wenden and J. Rubin, eds., *Learner Strategies and Language Learning*. Englewood Cliffs, N.J.: Prentice-Hall International.

O'Malley, J. M. and A. U. Chamot. 1990. *Learner Strategies in Second Language Acquisition*. Cambridge: Cambridge University Press.

O'Malley, J. M., A. U. Chamot, and C. Walker. 1987. "Some Applications of Cognitive Theory to Second Language Acquisition." *Studies in Second Language Acquisition* 9: 287-306.

Oxford, R. 1990. *Language Learning Strategies: What Every Teacher Should Know.* Rowley, MA.: Newbury House.

Pintrich, P. R. 1989. "The Dynamic Interplay of Student Motivation and Cognition in the College Classroom," in M. Maehr and C. Ames, eds., *Advances in Motivation and Achievement: Motivation Enhancing Environments.* Greenwich, CT: JAI Press.

Postovsky, V. 1974. "Effects of Delay in Oral Practice at the Beginning of Second Language Learning." *Modern Language Journal* 58: 229-34.

Rubin, J. 1990. "Improving Foreign Language Listening Comprehension." *Georgetown University Round Table.* Washington, DC: Georgetown University Press.

Rubin, J. 1987. "Learner Strategies: Theoretical Assumptions, Research History, and Typology," in A. Wenden and J. Rubin eds., *Learner Strategies in Language Learning.* Englewood Cliffs, NJ: Prentice-Hall International.

Rubin, J. and I. Thompson. 1994. *How to Be a More Successful Language Learner,* 2nd ed. Boston, MA: Heinle and Heinle.

Thompson, I. and J. Rubin. 1993. *Improving Listening Comprehension in Russian.* Research Report on Grant #PO17A00032, International Research and Studies Program, Department of Education, Washington, DC.

Shrum, J. and E. Glisan. 1994. *Teacher's Handbook.* Boston, MA: Heinle and Heinle.

Wenden, A. 1982. *The Processes of Self-Directed Learning: A Study of Adult Language Learners.* Doctoral Dissertation, New York: Teachers' College, Columbia University.

Wenden, A. 1991. *Learner Strategies for Learner Autonomy.* Englewood Cliffs, NJ: Prentice-Hall International.

Wenden, A. and J. Rubin, eds. 1987. *Learner Strategies in Language Learning.* Englewood Cliffs, NJ: Prentice-Hall International.

Willing, K. 1991. *Teaching How to Learn: Learning Strategies in ESL.* (Activity Worksheets and A Teachers Guide). Sydney, Australia: National Centre for English Language Teaching and Research. Also: San Diego, CA: Dominie.

Wong-Fillmore, L. 1976. "The Second Time Around: Cognitive and Social Strategies in Second Language Acquisition." Unpublished doctoral dissertation. Palo Alto, CA: Stanford University.

chapter 3

Instructional Technologies

James P. Pusack and Sue K. Otto

The University of Iowa

QUESTION 1: **What kinds of questions can teachers expect research on instructional technologies to answer?**

Discussion

First, as teachers, we must scale back our expectation that research studies will produce comprehensive answers to the broad questions of technology and language learning that we are accustomed to asking. While current research can offer us limited insights on specific issues, it cannot, at present, respond to the perennial overarching question, "Can technology improve language learning?" One of the explanations for this limitation is that researchers have tended to focus on technical issues that are often of little practical value to teachers. [Those who wish to go beyond the summary of research provided here are advised to read Dunkel, 1991, which provides an overview of computer-assisted language learning (CALL) research.]

Teachers, materials developers, and researchers should consider a number of factors when attempting to transfer the results of published studies to specific situations. These include the nature of the instructional setting, the nature of the CALL activities, and student characteristics and attitudes. Researchers also propose specific student characteristics that may be important in examining computer materials: age, expectations, ability, cognitive style, and effect. These concerns are the same ones teachers should raise as they attempt to determine how valid *any* research study is to their own situation (Jamieson and Chapelle, 1988; Chapelle and Jamieson, 1991).

QUESTION 2: What is the relationship between language acquisition research and CALL research?

Discussion

These two fields must work hand in hand. Few would disagree that it makes good sense to suggest that Second Language Acquisition (SLA) theory should influence the development of technology-based instructional materials. Likewise, it makes sense for SLA researchers to tap the vast resources potentially available through computer-assisted language learning (CALL) software. As both fields evolve and as practitioners become fully aware of the potential contributions of each, the synergy of blended CALL and SLA research and development will become a reality. The recordkeeping capabilities of CALL will allow SLA researchers to gather extensive data on the language learning process, such as how students use dictionaries or how students watch video. At the same time, the best insights of SLA research will continue to guide software developers in designing effective interactions. For example, a better under-standing of how students learn to read a second language can affect the activities offered to learners in a computer-based reading program. Chapelle offers another example of how computer research and SLA research can cross-fertilize each other. In analyzing the student-computer discourse in a lesson on grammar/paragraph development, she concludes: "Use of the same principles for student-computer interaction as for human interaction applies insights from linguistic research, thereby opening a novel perspective on unsolved human-factors issues in CALL" (pp. 221-22). Research of the type Chapelle describes may help overcome some of the obstacles of the past, such as technology studies that were too narrow in focus and application and attitude surveys that were inconclusive (Garrett, 1989; Chapelle, 1990; Doughty, 1991).

QUESTION 3: What kinds of writing software have been shown to improve students' writing? Is word processing valuable? Do elaborate "help systems" really help learners? And what about peer critiques via computer bulletin boards or networks?

Discussion

Recent literature on computer-based writing includes a number of studies that report the effects of requiring students to use a word processor for writing composi-tions. Researchers have observed a number of positive effects from this approach, both on student attitudes towards writing and revising and on the degree of attention students pay to the formal aspects of their writing (Li Nim Yu, 1990; Laing, van den Hoven, and Benessiano, 1991; Neu and Scarcella, 1991). One study (Laing et al., 1991) used a complex system to analyze compositions written by hand and those composed with a word processor. This study showed that students who used the word processor demonstrated greater control over French spelling and grammar, wrote more syntactically complex French, and were more motivated to eliminate errors in their writing.

Other studies have examined the effects of specific writing software programs. Craven (1988) studied the effectiveness of CUES, a computer program that prompts writers to reprocess or transform their knowledge while writing, rather than merely retelling information in the same way it was presented to them. Although the results of her formal experiment did not show that CUES had a significant effect on students' written products, the informal responses from the student questionnaires and critiques led her to draw an important conclusion about her research project—that she did not take into account important affective factors when setting up the experiments: "the students were reluctant to change established patterns, and they were not motivated to take chances in writing in English" (p. 60). The most important conclusion to be drawn here is that studies need to examine long-term changes in behavior in a context that explicitly addresses learner characteristics.

Kesner Bland, Noblitt, Armington, and Gay (1990) conducted a study in which students used *système-D*, a writing tool for French that combines a word processor with an interconnected set of language reference materials (a dictionary, a reference grammar with usage notes, and a notional/functional vocabulary and phrase reference). As first- and second-year students wrote compositions using this software program, the researchers analyzed the types of strategies these writers used in trying to construct meaning in French. From their data, the investigators concluded that the integrated approach to vocabulary and grammatical help like that used by *système-D* was an important feature to include in writing-tool software. More research on student use of comprehensive writing tools is required before we can generalize this result to all students at all levels of writing proficiency.

Dam, Legenhausen, and Wolff (1990) studied writing in small groups using a word processor. They looked at how the computer influences the interactional processes in front of the screen—whether students' attitudes towards the writing task are affected by the computer, and whether the computer influences writing strategies. Thirteen groups of two to four EFL students were observed and videotaped in various settings. The researchers concluded that the computer had a positive impact on students' attitudes towards the writing task and that the computer does influence students' writing strategies. In interpreting their results, they make this observation: "It is our contention that the screen text combines features of informal as well as formal registers. Its tentativeness and ephemeral quality is reminiscent of spontane-ously produced informal spoken language. This increases the students' willingness to take more risks, and their inhibitions against putting something down in writing are reduced" (p. 333).

Recent literature also includes a significant body of research that examines writing on computer networks. This form of communication combines aspects of both oral and written skills, and its introduction has fostered new modes of discourse that were not previously possible in classroom settings. Johnson (1991) provides a good overview of the issues of writing via computer networks—the need to plan tasks and settings, individual vs. pairs vs. groups, cooperative learning scenarios, and student empowerment with knowledge/status as experts. She describes several participation structures, including simultaneous conversation/discussion, peer review of composi-tions, collaborative writing, and delayed conversation/writing (pen-pals). However, when we look at various case studies of computer network communication, we find that each research project has a focal point somewhere along the continuum between pure writing (using a word processor to generate documents) and speaking (computer-based conversation, similar to CB radio conversation). Some computer network projects are better classified as "writing research." Other studies focus more on how computers can be used to improve or facilitate conversation.

Several studies have been conducted on peer review of written compositions that have been posted on networks (Esling, 1991; Sanaoui and Lapkin, 1992; Scinicariello, 1992; Sheppard, 1992). These studies analyze responses and reveal a number of common discourse traits of delayed written interchanges: Students felt encouraged to write extended comments; students paid attention to the formal aspects as well as the meaning of their messages; students were motivated to write for effective communi-cation and felt that the writing experience was more authentic than other kinds of classroom writing activities; and, if students were not acquainted with each other, communication topics always began with "get acquainted" information, followed by a shift to the targeted communication topic. In these studies, the teacher's role is primarily to manage (initiate and monitor) and critique student writing and written responses. Scinicariello observes that, although technology may change the teacher's *role*, it does not usually lessen the teacher's *work*. She notes "the enormous amount of time required to read, correct, and reread student submissions and to respond to spontaneous student inquiries. The use of the network essentially increased the class contact hours" (p. 188). In another study, Herrmann (1991) demonstrated the effective implementation of a newspaper-producing activity system that allowed American students of French to use the computer to write, revise, and comment on articles, or to communicate with others using electronic mail.

Finally, in the area of student attitudes toward word processing, Phinney (1991) used a questionnaire to examine attitudes toward writing on a computer among students enrolled in freshman ESL composition courses. The fourteen-week study indicated "that using a computer to write did reduce writing apprehension, improve attitudes, help students deal with deadlines, and enhance their perception of their ability to deal with complex material" (p. 198). This reduction of apprehension   appeared to have no impact, however, on students' tendency to focus on the formal aspects of their writing, rather than on the expression of meaning.

QUESTION 4: How can computers be used to improve conversational skills?

Discussion

A number of studies have examined the use of networks as communication tools. They conclude that computer-assisted discussion via networks has a number of positive features:

- more participation by each student is possible than in regular class discussion

- communication becomes more democratic, since the discussion cannot be dominated by more assertive students

- more students contribute to a single conversation

- students are not interrupted while expressing their thoughts

- students express themselves more freely because of the psychological distance the computer inserts between communicators

- emphasis on communication rather than form can lead to increased student confidence in using—both reading and producing—the second language.

Students intent on communication use a wide range of forms and constructions they might have otherwise avoided. The teacher is responsible for providing the questions or topics for discussion and for monitoring student communication. Even though observations abound regarding the nature of the discourse that takes place over the network, the pedagogical implications of this activity are not clear. Beauvois identified a number of provocative research questions related to network discussion of this kind, including questions about the degree to which writing of this type can improve speaking, reading, and composition skills. (Beauvois, 1992; Kelm, 1992; Sanaoui and Lapkin, 1992).

Computer simulations can also be used to stimulate conversation. Legenhausen and Wolff (1990) videotaped nine hours of student-peer interactions centered on the menu-operated adventure game GRANVILLE, in which students are asked to spend a five-day holiday on the French Atlantic coast. The researchers investigated (1) whether the simulation led to intensive communicative interactions between the participants, (2) what the linguistic and communicative quality of the interactions was in terms of discourse authenticity and acquisitional value, and (3) the extent to which the computer facilitated the participants' identification with their assigned roles and functions. The study concluded that, while the students were not fully immersed in the simulated environment, they engaged in authentic communication in order to discuss both the operation of the program and the tasks generated by the simulation. Teachers should take into account that computer-based simulations may stimulate conversation that is quite different from that found in classroom role-playing.

QUESTION 5: How can I decide if a piece of grammar software will be effective?

Discussion

Good luck! There is not very much evaluative research to guide teachers in this decision. A study by Bationo (1992) attempted to compare the effects of four types of feedback provided by a Macintosh-based French grammar tutorial program: spoken feedback, written feedback, written plus spoken feedback, no feedback. The results of the study showed that groups that received the combined written and spoken feedback and those who received spoken feedback only performed significantly better on immediate recall of the material than those who received written or no feedback. However, there was no significant difference in the performance of any of the groups in delayed recall of the material.

Robinson (1991) summarizes the results of a major 1985 study involving first-year Spanish high-school students who participated exclusively in CALL activities each day during a two-week field study. It was concluded that feedback in grammar lessons was most effective when software both indicated error locations and provided hints, when context-sensitive help was given in response to student requests, and when specific errors led to work on parallel items.

Other studies have surveyed student perceptions of the instructional value of certain design features of CALL exercises (Church, 1986; Fischer, 1989; Dhaif, 1990). These reports contain a number of observations about student preferences, many of which are not generalizable to CALL programs as a whole. However, the latter two studies had one observation in common: students' *perception* of the instructional value of CALL is not directly related to their levels of achievement.

QUESTION 6: Is there research to support the value of technologies in improving the receptive skills for individuals and small groups?

Discussion

Many of the current applications of language learning technology—audiotape, videotape, computer software, interactive videodisc—target the development of the receptive skills. The notion that videotape can enhance language learning is widely accepted in our profession and, in practical terms, video is one of the most accessible and affordable media available. Several recent studies comparing videotape-based or video-enhanced learning with traditional text-based approaches offer some insights about the benefits to be derived from video instruction. In two of these studies, researchers conducted classroom experiments with students of French to evaluate the impact of videotape instructional materials (*French in Action*) on skill development (Secules, Herron, and Tomasello, 1992; Herron, Morris, Secules, and Curtis, 1995). Their results showed that the experimental (*French in Action*) groups demonstrated greater skill in listening comprehension of conversations among primarily native speakers of French than those taught by traditional classroom methods (exercises and drills). The investigators found no statistical differences between groups on any other skill tests. On the final standardized writing test there was, however, a trend toward significance in favor of the experimental group (Herron et al., 1995). Another study compared the acquisition of specific grammar structures via the *French in Action* curriculum to that of a grammar-in-context approach (Ramsay, 1991). This study yielded somewhat contradictory results. No significant difference was found in overall test-score gains between the two groups; no significant difference was found between the improvement of the two groups; and, counter to expectations, no significant difference was found in the gains in listening comprehension (although the author expressed doubt about the validity of the instrument used to measure listening comprehension). However, significantly better grammar score gains were made by the *French in Action* group than by the control group. In fact, all studies successfully countered fears that students would not learn grammar in the video-based course.

A number of research projects have been conducted on the effectiveness of interactive videodisc (IAV) on listening comprehension and general achievement in language learning. Pioneering studies conducted during the 1980s at Brigham Young

University and the Air Force Academy indicate that students using interactive videodisc achieved higher gains in comprehension and retention of video content and in learning of vocabulary and grammar than those who used videotape (Smith, 1986; Chang and Smith, 1991). Although these studies support the value of interactive video as an instructional medium, a solid research base does not yet exist to guide either software designers or language teachers in integrating interactive video into the curriculum. However, as with all examples of research in new technologies, studies exploring specific aspects will begin to emerge in greater numbers for interactive video and full-fledged multimedia. We can expect, as is true of the following two studies, that research will focus not only on the learning benefits, but on practical issues, such as costs of hardware configurations and ergonomics—the coordination of machines and worksta-tion environments with human comfort and health factors.

Many teachers who have begun to explore multimedia soon find that one of their first decisions concerns the configuration of the student workstation. Cline (1991) conducted a study to compare students' learning of Spanish cultural materials using a workstation with video overlay (one-screen interactive video combining computer and video images) with those using a workstation with computer monitor and a separate video monitor (two-screen interactive video). Both groups of Spanish students made significant gains in their knowledge of Spanish culture from using the interactive video materials, but workstation configuration was not judged to be an important factor in determining student learning. Nevertheless, their final recommen-dation (because of price, ease of hardware setup, and efficiency of authoring) was the two-screen configuration.

Chang and Smith (1991a, 1991b) report the results of an experiment that evaluated the combined effect of cooperative learning (individuals vs. pairs) and interactive videodisc and its impact on reading achievement in beginning Spanish. There was no significant difference between individual and pair groups in understand-ing content and following the development of the story overall; working in pairs had no negative impact on learning—it was as effective as working alone. Also, less time was needed for pairs of students to reach the targeted level of performance. Individuals and pairs performed differently depending on the nature of the comprehension tasks. On the practical side, this study implies that when students can work in pairs rather than individually, fewer workstations need be installed in labs.

Logic tells us that there is a strong correlation between reading and listening. Development of vocabulary is critical to both; and, psycholinguistically, both involve a process of segmenting, synthesizing, and interpreting based on background knowl-edge and expectations. However, the real nature of the relationship between the two is still unknown. Research on this relationship is only now beginning to appear. In a study of elementary-school foreign language learners, Herron and Hanley (1992) report that utilizing video in the classroom facilitated the retention of cultural information in reading passages. Perhaps the most focused research investigating this relationship has been that on the use of captioned videotape materials. Studies of captioned videotape materials by Garza (1991), Neuman and Koskienen (1991), Hirose and Kamei (1992), and Markham (1992-93) all reported increases in listening comprehension and in vocabulary learning and control through the use of verbatim captioning of videotaped materials. In a major study by Garza, tests using both captioned and uncaptioned versions of authentic video materials in Russian and in English were administered to groups of advanced college students of Russian and ESL. Although the research supports the conventional wisdom that adding printed text to the audio of a video segment improves comprehension of the language, Garza makes a serious attempt to prove this assumption. Students were asked to tell what they understood and remembered about the video, thus allowing researchers to gauge the extent to which the language was assimilated by control and experimental groups. While the gains for experimental groups of both languages were positive, the comprehension and vocabulary control gains for the students of Russian were more striking that those of the ESL students—a difference the author attributed to the ESL students' more extensive experience with TV and movies. Garza maintains that students are able to attend to multiple channels of input; simultaneous text, audio, and video do not overload the student or tend to cancel each other out. He also concludes that reading effectively enhances listening: "The most significant conclusion suggested by this study is that captioning may help teachers and students of a foreign language bridge the often sizable gap between the development of skills in reading comprehension and listening comprehension, the latter usually lagging significantly behind the former" (p. 246).

The Hirose and Kamei study indicates that captions aided students' comprehension all levels of proficiency (especially at the word level), but that the level of sentence comprehension and of content interpretation was directly proportional to the level of the learner's proficiency. Finally, Markham examined the effects of captioned video material on ESL student comprehension. Subjects were advanced ESL students who completed a prior-knowledge-and-interest survey and a recall protocol. [See Barnett, this volume, for discussion of the recall protocol evaluation technique.] The study employed two videotaped segments with high vs. low levels of correlation between video context and words. It was found that the availability of captions was not significantly related to recall for the intermediate or the advanced students. Markham concludes that captions are not likely to play a dominant role in the comprehension of high intermediate and advanced ESL students when the video images strongly *reinforce* the audio component (p. 187). These results have helpful implications for development of interactive video and multimedia applications that allow selective display of transcript information.

What these studies on video captioning don't tell us is the effect this technique has on *building* better listening-comprehension skills. Does student viewing of captioned authentic videos increase their ability to comprehend other authentic videos which are uncaptioned? For example, in their experiments on video-based instruction, Secules et al. (1992) and Herron et al. (1995) tested students' comprehension of new, unfamiliar conversations between native speakers. Their research showed improved comprehension skills, in general, for students in the video-based instructional programs. Much more research is needed in this area to answer the important questions raised by these studies and to reveal the best strategies for using video and printed text to complement each other in the process of building students' receptive skills.

Relatively little research exists on the value of computer technology for the improvement of reading skills. Almost every computer-based activity involves reading, especially those based on network interactions; yet, reading has rarely been the focus of any assessment of these activities. Pederson (1986) studied whether having a reading passage available *during* testing affected reading comprehension, an issue that has important implications for computer-based reading software. Fourth-quarter university students of French were given authentic texts from recent French periodicals and asked to respond to both high- and low-level comprehension questions (questions requiring *synthesis of information* vs. those requiring *literal recognition*). Those students who had the passage available to them during the test were allowed to look ahead to the question before finishing the reading and to return to the passage while they attempted to answer the question. Those students who did not have the passage available to them during the test knew they could not look ahead to the questions. The results indicated that those for whom the passage was *unavailable* recalled more, regardless of the level of the question or of the student's verbal ability.

Certainly, we need much more research on such issues as the kind and availability of on-line help, the value of top-down vs. bottom-up reading strategies, what strategies are appropriate to different levels of learning, the interaction of different learner styles with technology-based learning, and the interaction between media (audio, video, graphics, text) and reading/listening comprehension.

QUESTION 7: Can interactive multimedia technology help us teach culture?

Discussion

There is little doubt that computers can effectively teach factual cultural information and expose students to other cultures through various information channels. Cline (1991) reported that students using interactive videodisc made gains in their knowledge of Spanish culture. Furstenberg's (1992) *A la Rencontre de Philippe* provides students a context for experiencing a number of aspects of authentic French culture. Hammadou (1991) reports that students who used the French communications system Minitel regarded it as a valuable resource for authentic data about French culture and as a good way to build cultural knowledge about France. The prospects for success in conveying culture through multimedia workstations seem very promising and warrant serious research.

QUESTION 8: What is the relationship between instructional technology and student motivation?

Discussion

There is a great deal of anecdotal "evidence" to support the claim that instructional technology is motivational to students. What is lacking here is substantial evidence that motivation to use the technology is directly related to achievement or to increased motivation to learn language (Church, 1986; Reese, Eastmond, and Sutherland, 1988; Dunkel, 1991b; Beauvois, 1992; Furstenberg, 1992; Sanaoui and Lapkin, 1992; Evans, 1993).

Some studies have looked at motivation in the opposite direction: the impact of motivation on learning through technology. Oxford et al. (1991, 1993) studied the factors that influence student achievement when instruction is delivered by satellite television. These researchers surveyed 107 American high-school students of elementary Japanese to test seven hypotheses about distance learning and learner characteristics, learning styles and strategies, motivation, and gender. They reached the conclusion that learner motivation and strategy use were determining factors in achievement via satellite programs:

As demonstrated by this investigation of a satellite-delivered Japanese language instruction program, student characteristics play a very important role in language achievement. In the satellite instruction context, these characteristics—especially motivation and learning strategy use--made a great difference, just as they have in studies conducted in the regular classroom. The more motivated the students were and the more they used learning strategies, the better their Japanese achievement was. (Oxford 1991: 46)

Stevens (1991) used a questionnaire to conduct a case study of student attitudes. His approach was exemplary, especially in the design of the questionnaire, the measurement of change over time, and the description of the software used. In this survey of 318 Arab students who used computers to study English in a self-access resource center setting, Stevens reports positive attitudes on a number of topics:

The results suggest that when the natural curiosity of students is coupled with a battery of CALL lessons configured to exploratory learning, the results can be gratifying, even for learners with a tendency toward rote learning. On the perennial question of whether computers are effective in teaching English, no claims are made; however, it appears that the students themselves generally feel they are gaining from using computers, and given this perception and overall positive attitudes, it is likely that they will want to use computers in attempting to do so. (Stevens, 1991: 298)

QUESTION 9: How can the present limitations of CALL be overcome? Is artificial intelligence the solution?

Discussion

Artificial intelligence (AI) refers to an area of research whose goal is to devise programs that respond to and interact with humans as *other humans* would do. The artificial intelligence portion of computer programs can serve as a natural-language processing system that responds to variation in human input, intelligently guess the meanings of the user, and check this understanding with the user. Artificial intelligence techniques, for example, will allow for more informative feedback to wrong answers than the standard "No, try again." AI will be able to suggest to students what was wrong and how to fix it without requiring software authors to anticipate all possible wrong answers in advance. The application of artificial intelligence to the production of FL learning materials has, by and large, kept up with the production of artificial intelligence software in other fields of instruction—that is to say, not much significant progress has been made. Open-ended, computer-based conversations are still a thing of the future, as are programs that can understand and critique student writing in a meaningful way. Programs that can analyze, understand, or interpret correct forms of language have been developed with some success; but, because such programs don't cope well with the incorrect language our students are likely to produce, they are of more interest to the theoretical linguist than to the developer of CALL materials. However, as researchers experiment with "parsers" that can diagnose and respond to specific *types* of student errors, their explorations may have important implications for future development of intelligent CALL software.

Nihongo-CALI, a Japanese program with 90 grammar exercises developed by Nagata (1993), is an excellent example of an artificial intelligence CALL program that utilizes a parser to provide sophisticated, intelligent error analysis and feedback to student responses. The major questions posed in Nagata's study were: Why do we need intelligent feedback? What kind of analysis and feedback should be provided to the student? The natural language processing of Nihongo-CALI focused on morphological, syntactic, and lexical components of the responses. The study compared *traditional* CALL error analysis and feedback based on pattern matching (what was wrong—missing, incomplete, extra words and parts of words) with intelligent analysis and feedback that included detailed explanations of why responses were wrong. Nagata's results suggested that "the traditional feedback may be as good as the intelligent feedback for helping learners to correct word-level errors (e.g., vocabulary and conjugation errors), while the intelligent feedback may be more helpful for understanding and correcting sentence-level errors, which involve more complex processing of knowledge" (p. 337).

Other than Nagata's work, no study could be found that investigated either the comparative effectiveness of an AI-driven program or a specific aspect of AI as a design feature. Part of the problem here is that the definition of AI is constantly changing. Computers now do many things that emulate human teachers at some low level (checking spelling; marking up wrong answers; providing a transcript for an unclear chunk of video; deciding which lesson to do next, based on student performance), but most AI-oriented developers are striving for something more. It is probably fair to say that all of the current effort is going into long-range basic (rather than applied) research to develop components of what will some day enhance CALL software.

For an enthusiastic vision of where AI, combined with hypermedia and simulation, may be going in the 1990s, readers should consult Underwood (1989), who classifies the aspirations for AI into three categories: intelligent tutoring systems, microworlds (simulations), and dialogue systems. Chapelle (1989) provides another excellent overview of AI as found in microworlds, intelligent grammar checkers, and intelligent tutoring systems. She recommends that teachers pay "careful attention to research and developments in AI, the psychological and linguistic aspects of language development, and research on current CALL practices" (p. 70). Teachers should be cautioned that AI, like multimedia, requires significant resources and introduces surprising complexities that will be extremely difficult to evaluate in terms of cost-effectiveness.

QUESTION 10: Why isn't there more research on language learning technology? Will today's research have any value for tomorrow's technologies?

Discussion

Jamieson and Chapelle (1988) give a remarkably concise response to those who decry the lack of research: "The closer the computer comes to teaching the student things that language teachers would like it to, the harder it is to measure whether a CALL activity has been successful" (p. 159). For this reason, carefully conducted descriptive research and case studies are extremely valuable. The lack of research on technology also derives from the state of our profession as a science, as described by Legenhausen and Wolff (1990):

> The evaluation of any teaching/learning material actually presupposes a theoretical framework, a theory of foreign language learning or acquisition, which would have to supply the criteria for the evaluative process. As is well-known, this state of affairs does not exist yet, and might not for decades to come. What we have to resort to and rely on at present, is the often referred to "collective wisdom of the profession." And again, there is not very much that practitioners and researchers can agree on (p. 1).

Teachers who have come to understand (perhaps the hard way) that there is no ideal methodology that will always fit all learners in all learning situations must also come to grips with the fact that no single research study will ever answer all their questions about technology.

Teachers and researchers alike must also consider the pace of technological change. For teachers trying to make decisions about *implementing* a given technology, studies that are more than 3-5 years old will not offer much help. Very few studies can be found that demonstrate the value of software packages now on the market. [See Kesner Bland et al., 1990; Ramsey, 1991; Furstenberg, 1992; Herron and Hanley, 1992; Secules et al., 1992; and Herron et al., 1995.] Nevertheless, it is increasingly possible to find both qualitative and descriptive studies that provide *insights* into the features of good CALL technologies and into exemplary ways of implementation. These insights will have value for developers and users of future technologies.

QUESTION 11: **If relevant research is not available, how should I make decisions about technology? How can I decide if a given technology is cost-effective? What shall I tell those who ask me for evidence that CALL is worth the cost?**

Discussion

Here are a few concrete recommendations:

    ✿   Familiarize yourself with some representative studies, such as those included here.

    ✿   Talk to people who are using CALL in settings similar to your own.

    ✿   Ask publishers of software for any relevant studies or lists of adopters.

    ✿   Remember that some technologies are good simply because they offer access to materials your students would not otherwise have.

    ✿   Invite your administrators to read some or all of the items in the list of references that accompanies this chapter; show them that there *is* research.

    ✿   Accept the fact that if you try to implement a new technology, you are bound to be ahead of the research.

    ✿   If all else fails, become the researcher and produce the research you cannot find.

Bibliography

Bationo, B. D. 1992. "The Effects of Three Feedback Forms on Learning Through a Computer-Based Tutorial." *CALICO Journal* 10,1: 45-52.

Beauvois, M. H. 1992. "Computer-Assisted Classroom Discussion in the Foreign Language Classroom: Conversation in Slow Motion." *Foreign Language Annals* 25: 455-64.

Chang, K. R. and W. F. Smith. 1991a. "CALL/IVD Workstations: Towards a Rationale for Their Use in Cooperative Learning Environments," in M. D. Bush, A. Slaton, M. Verano, and M. E. Slayden, eds., *Interactive Videodisc: The "Why" and the "How"*. CALICO Monograph Series, vol. 2. Provo, UT: CALICO.

Chang, K. R. and W. F. Smith. 1991b. "Cooperative Learning and CALL/IVD in Beginning Spanish: An Experiment." *Modern Language Journal* 75: 205-11.

Chapelle, C. 1989. "Using Intelligent Computer-Assisted Language Learning." *Computers and the Humanities* 23: 59-70.

Chapelle, C. 1990. "The Discourse of Computer-Assisted Language Learning: Toward a Context for Descriptive Research." *TESOL Quarterly* 24: 199-225.

Chapelle, C. and J. Jamieson. 1991. "Internal and External Validity Issues in Research on CALL Effectiveness," in P. Dunkel, ed., *Computer-Assisted Language Learning and Testing*. New York: Newbury House.

Church, D. M. 1986 "Textbook Specific Computer Exercises for Elementary French Students." *Modern Language Journal* 70: 251-57.

Cline, W. J. 1991. "Interactive Video: One Monitor or Two?" *The IALL Journal of Language Learning Technologies* 24,1: 25-35.

Craven, M. L. 1988. "Evaluating CUES: Some Problems and Issues in Experimental CALL Research." *CALICO Journal* 5,3: 51-64.

Dam, L., L. Legenhausen, and D. Wolff. 1990. "Text Production in the Foreign Language Classroom and the Word Processor." *System* 18: 325-334.

Dhaif, H. A. 1990. "Computer Assisted Language Learning: A Client's View." *CALICO Journal* 7,4: 67-81.

Doughty, C. 1991. "Theoretical Motivations for IVD Software Research and Development," in M. D. Bush, A. Slaton, M. Verano, and M. E. Slayden, eds., *Interactive Videodisc: The "Why" and the "How"*. CALICO Monograph Series, vol. 2. Provo, UT: CALICO.

Dunkel, P. 1991a. "Computerized Testing of Nonparticipatory L2 Listening Comprehension Proficiency: An ESL Prototype Development Effort." *Modern Language Journal* 75: 64-73.

Dunkel, P. 1991b. "The Effectiveness Research on Computer-Assisted Instruction and Computer-Assisted Language Learning," in P. Dunkel, ed., *Computer-Assisted Language Learning and Testing*. New York: Newbury House.

Esling, J. H. 1991. "Researching the Effects of Networking: Evaluating the Spoken and Written Discourse Generated by Working with CALL," in P. Dunkel, ed., *Computer-Assisted Language Learning and Testing*. New York: Newbury House.

Evans, M. 1993. "*Nicolas*: Using *Hypercard* with Intermediate-Level French Learners." *System* 21: 213-29.

Fischer, R. A. 1989. "Instructional Computing in French: The Student View." *Foreign Language Annals* 22: 79-90.

Furstenberg, G. 1992. "Making the Connection I: Interactive Videodisc Technology in the Language Lab and Interactivities in the Classroom. *A la Rencontre de Philippe*: A Case Study," in I. Shinjo, K. Landahl, M. MacDonald, K. Noda, S. Ozeki, T. Shiozawa, and M. Sugiura, eds., *Proceedings of The Second International Conference on Foreign Language Education and Technology*. Kasugai, Aichi: Language Laboratory Association of Japan and International Association for Learning Laboratories.

Garza, T. J. 1991. "Evaluating the Use of Captioned Video Materials in Advanced Foreign Language Learning." *Foreign Language Annals* 24: 239-58.

Garrett, N. 1989. "The Synergism of Technology and Theory in Classroom Second Language Acquisition Research," in J. E. Alatis, ed., *Georgetown University Round Table on Languages and Linguistics 1989. Language Teaching, Testing, and Technology: Lessons from the Past with a View Toward the Future*. Washington, DC: Georgetown University Press.

Hammadou, J. 1991. "Student Interaction with Minitel Telecommunications." *The IALL Journal of Language Learning Technologies* 24,2: 7-18.

Herrmann, F. 1991. "Instrumental and Agentive CALL in Learning French as a Foreign Language." Eric Document 332545. Washington, DC: ERIC Clearinghouse on Higher Education.

Herron, C., M. Morris, T. Secules, and L. Curtis. 1995. "A Comparison Study of the Effects of Video-based Versus Text-based Instruction in the FL Classroom." *French Review* 68: forthcoming.

Herron, C. and J. Hanley. 1992. "Using Video to Introduce Children to a Foreign Culture." *Foreign Language Annals* 25,5: 419-26.

Hirose, K. and S. Kamei. 1992. "Effects of English Captions: How to Present Films in EFL Classrooms," in I. Shinjo, K. Landahl, M. MacDonald, K. Noda, S. Ozeki, T. Shiozawa, and M. Sugiura, eds., *Proceedings of The Second International Conference on Foreign Language Education And Technology.* Kasugai, Aichi: Language Laboratory Association of Japan and International Association for Learning Laboratories.

Jamieson, J. and C. Chapelle. 1988. "Using CALL Effectively: What Do We Need to Know about Students?" *System* 16:151-62.

Johnson, D. M. 1991 "Second Language and Content Learning with Computers: Research in the Role of Social Factors," in P. Dunkel, ed., *Computer-Assisted Language Learning and Testing.* New York: Newbury House.

Kelm, O. R. 1992. "The Use of Synchronous Computer Networks in Second Language Instruction: A Preliminary Report." *Foreign Language Annals* 25: 441-54.

Kesner Bland, S., J. S. Noblitt, S. Armington, and G. Gay. 1990. "The Naive Lexical Hypothesis: Evidence from Computer-Assisted Language Learning." *Modern Language Journal* 74: 440-50.

Laing, D., A. van den Hoven, and V. Benessiano. 1991. "L'emploi du traitement de texte dans un cours universitaire de première année portant sur la littérature française." *The Canadian Modern Language Review* 47: 477-84.

Legenhausen, L. and D. Wolff. 1990. "CALL in Use—Use of CALL: Evaluating CALL Software." *System* 18:1-13.

Li Nim Yu, K. 1990. "Writing with Pen or Computer? A Study on ESL Secondary School Learners." Eric Document 322720. Washington, DC: ERIC Clearinghouse on Higher Education.

Markham, P. L. 1992-93. "Captioned Television Videotapes: Effects of Visual Support on Second Language Comprehension." *Journal of Educational Technology Systems* 21: 183-93.

Nagata, N. 1993. "Intelligent Computer Feedback for Second Language Instruction." *Modern Language Journal* 77: 330-39.

Neu, J. and R. Scarcella. 1991. "Word Processing in the ESL Writing Classroom: A Survey of Student Attitudes," in P. Dunkel, ed., *Computer-Assisted Language Learning and Testing.* New York: Newbury House.

Neuman, S. B. and P. Koskienen. 1991. "Captioned Television as 'Comprehensible Input': Effects of Incidental Word Learning from Context for Language Minority Students." Eric Document 332538. Washington, DC: ERIC Clearinghouse on Higher Education.

Oxford, R., Y. Park-Oh, S. Ito, and M. Sumrall. 1991. "Learning a Language by Satellite Television: What Influences Student Achievement?" *System* 21: 31-48

Oxford, R., Y. Park-Oh, S. Ito, and M. Sumrall. 1993. "Japanese by Satellite: Effect of Motivation, Language Learning Styles and Strategies, Gender, Course Level, and Previous Language Learning Experience on Japanese Language Achievement." *Foreign Language Annals* 26: 359-71.

Pederson, K. M. 1986. "An Experiment in Computer-Assisted Second-Language Reading." *Modern Language Journal* 70: 36-41.

Phinney, M. 1991. "Computer-Assisted Writing and Writing Apprehension in ESL Students," in P. Dunkel, ed., *Computer-Assisted Language Learning and Testing*. New York: Newbury House.

Ramsay, R. 1991. "*French in Action* and the Grammar Question." *The French Review* 65: 255-66.

Reese, G. L., J. N. Eastmond, Jr., and R. Sutherland. 1988. "Integrated Videodisc for Intensive Spanish Language Learning." *CALICO Journal* 6,1: 69-81.

Robinson, G. L. 1991. "Effective Feedback Strategies in CALL: Learning Theory and Empirical Research," in P. Dunkel, ed., *Computer-Assisted Language Learning and Testing*. New York: Newbury House.

Sanaoui, R. and S. Lapkin. 1992. "A Case Study of an FSL Senior Secondary Course Integrating Computer Networking." *The Canadian Modern Language Journal* 48: 525-52.

Secules, T., C. Herron, and M. Tomasello. 1992. "The Effect of Video Context on Foreign Language Learning." *Modern Language Journal* 76: 480-90.

Sheppard, M. and S. Scinicariello. 1992. "Computer Networks for Foreign Language: On Campus and Around the World," in I. Shinjo, K. Landahl, M. MacDonald, K. Noda, S. Ozeki, T. Shiozawa, and M. Sugiura, eds., *Proceedings of The Second International Conference on Foreign Language Education and Technology*. Kasugai, Aichi: Language Laboratory Association of Japan and International Association for Learning Laboratories.

Smith, W. F., ed. 1989. *Modern Technology in Foreign Language Education: Applications and Projects*. Lincolnwood, IL: National Textbook.

Stevens, V. 1991. "A Study of Student Attitudes toward CALL in a Self-Access Student Resource Centre." *System* 19: 289-99.

Underwood, J. "On the Edge: Intelligent CALL in the 1990s." *Computers and the Humanities* 23: 71-84.

chapter 4

Teaching for Cultural Diversity

Genelle Morain
University of Georgia

QUESTION 1: At faculty meetings we hear about the current emphasis on "multicultural education." What exactly *is* multicultural education?

Discussion

Most educators who say they are practicing "multicultural education" subscribe to the concept of *cultural pluralism*, which uses the metaphor of the tossed salad or the patchwork quilt to describe the United States.

Cultural pluralism honors diversity, respects differences, and grants to every individual the right to participate in all aspects of society, while retaining individual uniqueness. But cultural pluralism itself has been used to describe at least four different configurations, which William Newman tried to clarify by representing each one as a different equation (Sleeter and Grant, 1994: 177):

1) $A + B + C = A$ (with A, B, and C representing different social groups and the dominant group being represented by A). This equation describes the process of *assimilation*, where the behavioral patterns and values of minority groups are assimilated into those of the majority group.

2) $A + B + C = D$ (with A, B, and C synthesizing into a new and distinct group represented by the *amalgam* D).

3) $A + B + C = A + B + C$ (with A, B, and C representing separate groups that keep their own identities over time). This formula depicts classic cultural pluralism.

4) $A + B + C = A_1 + B_1 + C_1$ (where the subscript 1 represents the shared culture which has become a *part* of each unassimilated co-culture). This formula depicts the theory of modified cultural pluralism, which holds that the shared culture (for our purposes, American) should be taught to all, but that the unique aspects of each co-culture should be recognized and also taught to all.

There is every reason to believe that while students are learning about the culture of the people whose language we are teaching, they can also be learning about their own culture and its relationship to other cultures in the school. At the same time, they can be acquiring an awareness of different modes of thinking, feeling, and behaving. They can carry away from our classes not only the ability to communicate with those who speak a *foreign* language, but an enhanced ability to communicate more sensitively with those who speak their *own* language. To enable students to gain these benefits, however, we as teachers need to strengthen our own understanding of the diversity in American classrooms and of the opportunities this diversity presents for broadening the dimensions of culture teaching.

QUESTION 2:   While teaching foreign cultures, we often encounter generalizations and stereotypes. How should we address this issue in the classroom?

Discussion

In our enthusiasm for imparting cultural information, we hear ourselves telling our students, "Well, the Spanish like to..." or "The Japanese always..." or "The typical Roman would..." Then we stop short and glance nervously over our shoulder to glimpse an Unforgiveable Stereotype sneering behind us. One way to foil this intruder would be to avoid all commitment. For instance, if a student posed a question such as, "Are the French optimistic or pessimistic?" the teacher might respond, "Well, some French are optimistic all of the time; others are optimistic on occasion; while others are rarely optimistic." Such a response makes it clear that a generalization cannot delineate the degree of optimism or pessimism of every French person. Indeed, a generalization cannot speak with confidence about every member of **any** group. It is critically important that our students understand this. Acquiring a healthy suspicion of generalizations and stereotypes is indeed one of the gifts they can receive in foreign language class that will serve them well across the curriculum.

Scholars used to differentiate between "stereotype" and "generalization," arguing that stereotypes were group descriptions that were based on folk belief and insufficient evidence, while generalizations were statements about groups that were formulated after careful research. Today, writers often use the terms almost interchangeably, although a more negative image clings to stereotype, while the terms "careful" or "reasonable" may precede use of the word generalization (Brislin, 1993).

Both stereotypes and generalizations are shortcuts, in that they permit us to rapidly organize information into categories. Both terms refer to beliefs about groups of people without acknowledging that individual characteristics within the group may be scattered along a wide continuum. When we accept a stereotype, we tend to interact with members of a given group according to the label attached. "Watch out for teenage drivers," we are warned. "They are wild and reckless." With this stereotype in the back of my mind, I might refuse to loan my new car to the eighteen-year-old next door who needed to run an errand across town at rush hour. In reality, that teenager may have earned the highest score ever received in the driver's training course; but "wild and reckless" is what sticks in my mind. Insurance companies uniformly charge a hefty extra fee when a teenager begins to drive the family vehicle. Stereotype, or careful generalization? It is difficult indeed to force ourselves to remember that individual differences exist in every group.

In their comparative study of five cultures, anthropologists Kluckhohn and Strodtbeck (1961) concluded that people of all cultures struggle to find solutions to a limited number of problems common to all human beings; and that although different cultures evolve different solutions, the variability is not limitless: all solutions lie within the same range of possibilities. The most important point for our discussion is that, while all alternative solutions to these common problems can be found in every culture, they are *preferred differentially.* That is, while individuals and small groups within the culture may opt for a variety of different solutions, there is usually a preferred solution favored by a large number of the members of the culture. For us as classroom teachers, this means we should never lose sight of the fact that individual students may not fit a group description, but a knowledge of *general cultural and linguistic preferences of the group* may help us recognize student difficulties and establish a learning climate that benefits all students maximally. [For discussion of the application of the Kluckhohn Model to the teaching of culture in a college Spanish class, see Ortuno, 1991.]

Avoiding generalizations and stereotypes altogether is probably an unrealistic goal. It is impossible to outlaw a cognitive process that enables the human brain to perform the very useful function of clumping information into categories. What we, as teachers, can do is help our students recognize a stereotype when they hear one, see one, or give voice to one. It is the *unidentified* stereotype that is dangerous. Once a stereotype is identified, students must:

1) Analyze their own response to the stereotype: Was it one of automatic acceptance, based on prior cultural conditioning?

2) Examine the content of the stereotype critically.

3) Remind themselves that there exists in every group a possibility for wide variation in values, behaviors, and beliefs.

4) Be willing to discard the stereotype if evidence points to a different reality.

Unfortunately, the *unexamined* stereotype solidifies into a stubborn belief that resists change and attracts the strong emotional baggage we call prejudice. A prejudice is a *feeling*, not a fact. When we help our students realize that all statements which assign characteristics to groups must be thoughtfully examined, we are also helping them to diminish prejudice.

The opportunity to examine stereotypes and the roles they play in interpersonal communication occurs with great frequency in the foreign language class. The increased awareness of their own and others' responses to stereotyping is a valuable understanding that students can carry into all aspects of their lives.

QUESTION 3: How can we help our students avoid the tendency to look at another culture (C2) through the perceptual lens of their own culture (C1)?

Discussion

First of all, we must remind ourselves that the life experiences of most of our students have *given* them no other perceptual lens than their own. With our help, the process of learning another language and culture can supply them with that second lens.

In learning a foreign language, the **function of language** is to communicate—to declare, to question, to request, etc. The various **forms of language**—sounds, words, grammatical constructions, gestures—are combined in intricate but systematic ways to achieve that communication. These same concepts—function and form—are also the components of culture. The **functions of culture** include the universal needs that every society must satisfy, such as attaining food, shelter, stability. Functions of culture also include meanings and purposes. The **forms of culture** are developed to enable the members of the culture to perform or fulfill the functions. They include *tangible* forms such as utilitarian and expressive objects, foods, means of transportation, and dwellings. They also include *intangible* forms—laws, patterns of behavior, beliefs, and values (Sapir, 1951; Byrnes, 1991; Galloway, 1992).

Because we grow up immersed in our own culture—absorbing its values, conforming to its rules of conduct, and feeling comfortable with its various functions and forms—this way of life becomes, for us, The Right Way. When we are confronted with another culture, we judge it by the only standards we know—our own. We automatically superimpose our own cultural constructs on the forms and functions of the other culture. The strange new solutions to fulfilling life's needs which work effectively for the other culture may baffle, irritate, or amuse us; its different forms of behavior may strike us as quaint at best, immoral at worst. Even more disconcerting, its seemingly *familiar* forms and functions may turn out to be used at unexpected times to accomplish startling results. As a final disorienting factor, some of our own most cherished functions and forms *may not even exist* in the second culture. For example, as Galloway (1992) points out:

> In U.S. society...it is common to speak of a "competitive instinct." Competition as a motivating need is manifested through countless forms, from sports activities to education and business practices to acquisition of material goods. Yet the notion may be as alien to another culture as it is elemental to the American. Notions so powerful in U.S. culture—privacy, security, freedom, control—may be barely functional in another culture, even altogether undesirable. (pp. 90-91)

Tolkein (1979), lecturing at the Fife Folklore Conference at Utah State University, told his predominately European-American, competition-oriented audience about the Navajo woman who was watching a ball game on television for the first time. She observed in perplexed silence for awhile, then asked, "Why don't they give that ball to the boys on the other side so that everyone can have a chance to play?"

In a recent study of high school learners of Spanish, Hall and Ramirez (1993) conclude:

> For a change in cultural perceptions to occur, learners need to become cognizant of their own identities and those of others as both individuals and as cultural beings. Otherwise they cannot reflect upon or respond to other cultural groups, recategorize their cultural perceptions, and achieve successful intercultural communication. (p. 617)

These are the kinds of understandings we must help our students acquire: a realization that other cultures have worked out their own ways to satisfy the basic needs that all humans share, and—of equal importance—a more profound knowledge of the nature of their own culture.

To illustrate the degree of our own cultural conditioning and the complex form/ function networks that we establish as a culture, we need only look at our schools and classrooms. While **learning** is a function that exists in every culture, it is a conceptually different phenomenon from one culture to another. In the United States, the function of learning is linked to other highly esteemed notions, such as work and success. There are also certain **forms** that correspond to this function in the U.S, behaviors that we not only associate with the function of learning, but that we take as signs that this function is being fulfilled: arrive on time, raise your hand for permission to talk, don't run in the halls, stay in your seat until the bell rings.

The culture of our schools expects conformity to the rules, just as the cultures of the schools of every nation do. The rules, of course, are different from nation to nation and from school to school within every nation; but the majority of schools in the United States can still be recognized by these practices or cultural **forms**:

1) **U.S. classroom expectations for paying attention:** When the teacher is talking, listen. Look directly at the teacher, but not in a hostile or challenging way. If the teacher is talking directly to you in a one-to-one mode, nod your head to indicate agreement and make appropriate response sounds of a positive nature in your throat (regional variant: in the South, say "Yes, Ma'am/Sir" from time to time). Do not look down or to the side, a sure indication of either guilt or boredom, both equally certain to incur the displeasure of the teacher.

2) **U.S. classroom expectations for interaction:** Show interest by asking questions. Volunteer (to put your homework on the board, to read your poem, to take part in a learning activity). When assigned to a small group, cooperate. When there is a discussion, participate (but don't ramble; get to the point).

3) **U.S. classroom expectations for high achievement:** Certain attributes are more highly favored by teachers than others. Speed and accuracy, in combination, are high on the list. They are required for high scores on standardized tests. They are also expected when answering teachers' questions; long "wait times" for responses slow the pace of the class and make teachers jittery. Self-motivation is looked upon with approval; to be pegged as a "self-starter" is a real plus. Teachers perceive this as evidence of an independent, resourceful nature, much prized in our culture. For example, when you are writing a book review, most teachers

expect you to express your own ideas in addition to those of the author; "having an opinion of your own" is meritorious. So is "having a good attitude." Perseverance is encouraged; trial and error are seen as healthy manifestations of the optimistic American approach "If at first you don't succeed, try, try again." Top-ranked among all the attributes, however, are the intellectual abilities traditionally favored by no-nonsense, product-oriented Americans: analytical reasoning, hypothesis testing, and problem-solving.

Mainstream teachers and students, if not instantly able to articulate these expectations of the school culture, would nevertheless be quick to recognize them. It is the *diversity* of our student populations which offers many examples of the dangers of judging C2 culture with C1 eyes. Our own classrooms are increasingly enriched with students from various Asian cultures, from Africa and the Middle East, and from many Spanish-speaking nations. Our students also represent different co-cultures within the United States—African American and Native American, among others. Since the culture of the school was derived primarily from the expectations of white, middle-class America, students from co-cultures, as well as more recent immigrants, sometimes find themselves confronted with the problem of *cultural discontinuity.* This notion holds that when there is a mismatch between the culture of the home and the culture of the school, there will be misunderstandings between the teacher and the students, reflected in interpersonal relations, in the kinds of learning activities assigned, and in the students' performance of the assignments (Au, 1992). Unfortu-nately, examples of this mismatch abound.

Robinson (1988) cites an instance of how different ways of speaking contribute to cross-cultural misunderstanding between students and teachers from different cultural backgrounds. English uses three levels of pitch for normal conversation and a fourth level for excitement and anger. Spanish uses two levels for normal conversation and the third is for excitement. Young Spanish-speaking children in a class may thus perceive an Anglo teacher as excited, angry, or shouting when this is not at all the case. Corroborative evidence of the interface between language and cultural response is supplied by researchers Hernandez and Santiago (1983), who analyzed teachers' disapproval behavior and found that Latino teachers were governed by the Puerto Rican value of *respeto* (an intense form of respect) when displaying disapproval. They used courtesy and indirect forms such as conditional tense, please and thank you, appealing more to group control than to individual control. European American teachers, in contrast, were much more direct in making their disapproval felt—they spoke to individuals in a terse, no-nonsense style. The Latino children in the classes studied interpreted these Anglo behaviors in a negative way and felt hurt and rejected.

Sometimes misunderstandings may arise because the connotations and cultural value of words differ from one culture to another. Kramsch (1991) cites the American student of German who asks the teacher, "How do you say *challenge* in German?", a question that cannot be addressed by mere direct translation:

> Whereas German culture considers difficulties as *Hindernisse* (obstacles), *Aufgaben* (tasks), *Probleme* (problems) or even *Schicksale* (destinies), American culture, born from a different history, values obstacles as tests of strength, things or events to be surmounted, overcome, beaten, and won, as on a football field. The American student first has to be sensitized to the ideological value of the word *challenge* in his/her own culture: the pioneer spirit of white America's beginnings, the inflation of the word in the last ten years, when entrepreneurship is praised to the point where even such catastrophes as the oil spills in Alaska are called "environmental challenges," and when the official term for such personal tragedies as physically handicapped persons is now "the physically challenged" (p. 196).

Robinson (1988) also provides an example of how communication can easily break down in the school setting because of a mismatch of cultural assumptions. A teacher sent a note home requesting that the parents of a Vietnamese child come to the school for a conference. But instead of the parents, the oldest son in the family arrived for the appointment. This annoyed the teacher, who wanted to talk about the student's problems with the *responsible* members of the family, whom the teacher assumed were the parents, not the son. In Vietnamese homes, however, when the father is dead (as was the case in this instance), it is the eldest son, not the mother, who takes over. Unaware of this difference, the teacher jumped to the conclusion that the mother was unconcerned about her child's problems in school.

Interesting differences in perceptions of work and play also exist across cultures. Galloway (1992) discusses the struggles a group of American students had in attempting to understand the French concept of *leisure* as it was presented in a cultural note. Able to draw only on their own cultural background in which, as Galloway puts it, "Work ... is what life is all about," the Americans were nonplussed to read that the French routinely take a two-hour lunch break, don't discuss their jobs at night, never take work home on weekends, are granted by law a minimum of five weeks of vacation per year, and give their leisure time equal priority to their job. With no other source to supply C2 perspectives, the students superimposed their C1 framework on the other culture and ended up with the dubious satisfaction of reinforcing another stereotype: "The French are lazy."

Kochman (1989) discusses other cross-cultural differences in attitudes toward work and play, focusing on African Americans and white Americans. Although mainstream whites stress the concept of individuality, when they become a member of a team, they are expected to downplay their own egos and work instead for the successful functioning of the group. This mental set regards organized work and play as serious—a thing that is to be structured, scheduled, and undertaken systematically. At the corporate level or on the ball field, a good team player knows the game plan and concentrates on following it. African American cultural style, on the other hand, is derived from a world view that sees *change* rather than *set* as the prevailing order. The key word is *reflex*, for if one is to survive the changes, improvisation and spontaneity are essential. Within this tradition, the individual performer is given liberty to respond creatively to whatever change comes along, to even generate a new plan, devise a new script: "I'm not a prize fighter; I'm a *surprise* fighter" (p. 267).

QUESTION 4: Have any studies shown differences in the way people learn across cultures?

Discussion

Some researchers have focused on differences in learning styles across cultures (primarily with elementary-school children) in the attempt to identify certain ranges or tendencies in the ways different peoples approach different types of learning tasks. Certain caveats must accompany such studies, however. Researchers, too, are profoundly influenced (and limited by) their own cultural framework of values in the notions they choose to focus on and the forms or behaviors they select for observation and measurement. For example, the two terms "field independent" and "field dependent" are often used to describe two common and contrastive learning styles (Witkin, 1962). Learners characterized as field independent are said to be self-motivated and to prefer working alone. They enjoy solving problems, testing hypotheses, and focusing on details. Field independence is strongly characterized by analytic reasoning. Field dependent learners, on the other hand, are said to dislike competitive situations and to prefer working cooperatively in small groups. They enjoy discussion, sharing personal anecdotes, and focusing on the big picture. The term global reasoning characterizes the field dependent learner. Some researchers claim that Hispanic, African American, and Native American children tend to be field dependent in their learning styles, while European Americans tend to be field independent (Hale-Benson, 1982; Ramirez and Castaneda, 1974). Such contrasts, however, can lead to rigid dichotomies and misunderstandings. Nieto (1992) cites a disturbing story recounted by a researcher who found that teachers were using the "cooperative" label from the field dependent category to make discriminatory decisions regarding Hispanic students in their classes. If there were not enough books to go around, non-Hispanic students received single copies, while Hispanic students were required to share, on the assumption that they would enjoy the contact with a classmate. When opportunities for solo performances in plays or other leadership roles came around, they were given to non-Hispanic students with the "justification" that Hispanic students would not be comfortable in such independent roles. The teachers were not only ignoring the very likely possibility of field independent learners among the Hispanic students, they were also imprinting their own C1 "forms" on the notion of cooperativeness and using preconceptions to justify unsatisfactory solutions.

Certainly cultures, with their distinctive world views, shape the learning styles of their children before they even arrive at school. Brown (1991) discusses the findings of a researcher at the University of Northern Arizona, R. Rhodes, who studied patterns of natural learning among southwestern Native American tribes. Rhodes pointed out that from an early age Indian children are given significant responsibility at home—caring for younger siblings and tending herds of animals, often for days at a time. In contrast, at school they are given virtually no responsibility. At home they learn in natural context, first observing adults who perform a task, then going off alone to practice the task themselves. When children feel secure enough to share their developing skill with friends, they go to them and work together to improve still further. Only when confident that the skill is under firm control does a child demonstrate his/her ability to an adult. The adult observes quietly, but without fanfare or accolades. The contrast with school is stark, especially in the aspect of performance. Indian children are not conditioned to perform in public on cue at an adult's bidding. As Rhodes puts it,

> Indians take a long time observing a situation and thinking about it.... The trial and error approach to problem solving makes no sense on the reservation. If you're a long way from home with the herd, and the weather is looking bad, and you're running out of food, you have to decide the right thing to do the first time. There's little margin for error. (Quoted in Brown, 1991: 69)

With most teachers accustomed to providing a 5- to 8-second wait-time before requiring a response to a question, the 45 to 90 seconds preferred by many Native American students for understanding a question and formulating a response is rarely allowed. Instead, the teacher often interprets the extended silence as inability to give the correct answer and calls on somebody else.

Wong Fillmore (1986), in a study of how Chinese and Hispanic children learned English in third and fifth grade classrooms, found that instructional variables affected oral language development differently according to the cultural backgrounds and the initial level of English proficiency of the learners. For the Hispanic children, frequent opportunities to interact with other children in the new language proved to aid both comprehension and production skills, regardless of their initial level of proficiency. But for the Chinese children, interacting with peers was of little help until they had gained a high enough level of control to feel confident in using the language with English-speaking classmates. The Hispanic children wanted activities which were clearly related to some meaningful whole. The Chinese children, however, did not mind assignments calling for drill and practice, no matter how tedious or meaningless. They compensated for the lack of real meaning in their lessons by viewing the skills they were acquiring as the real substance of school. As Wong Fillmore concluded, "Their culture, in fact, may even place a higher value on skill development for children than it does on meaningful experience and self expression" (p. 479). She recounts an incident in which she observed some Asian kindergarten children lined up after school, waiting for a bus. Some were sorting through the papers they had produced that day, saving to take home the pages on which they had practiced their letters and numbers, and tossing into the trash can all the papers with their drawings. When asked why they were throwing away "all the good stuff" (the pictures in which they had expressed their fancies and emotions), the children declared that the pictures were not "real school work" and explained that their parents wanted them to bring home only the papers that represented "real work."

Common American classroom practices can be confusing to international students. Asian children are frequently bewildered by the spontaneous behaviors of their peers in American classrooms, which they interpret as disrespect for authority. They are appalled by the expectation that they should volunteer answers and information, behavior which they view as immodest (Cheng, 1987). Even a friendly teacher's use of positive reinforcement may be rejected, as this quote from a case study of a young Vietnamese refugee attests:

> Sometimes, the English teachers, they don't understand about us. If my English is not good... some Americans say, "You're doing a good job. You're doing great. Everything is great." ...My culture is different.... They say, "You have to do better." So sometimes when I do something not good, and my teachers say, "Oh, you did great," I don't like it.... I want the truth better. (Nieto, 1992: 143)

Heath's (1982) seminal study on styles of questioning illuminated yet another difference in cross-cultural communication. The Anglo teachers working with African American children in the schools of a largely black community were discovered to be using a questioning pattern that was alien to the home environment of the children. The teachers were asking questions to which they already knew the answers. These "known answer" questions are frequently used by white middle class parents to coach their children in how to label objects and how to name the attributes of people and things. ("Can you point to the turtles, Becky? What color is the big turtle?") But African American adults do not usually ask this type of question. Instead, they pose analogy-type questions which encourage children to compare one thing to another. ("What do you think of when you see that rubber tire, Amahl?") When Heath worked with the white teachers to modify the questioning style they habitually employed in the classroom, the results were immediate and positive. The African American children responded with new enthusiasm to the familiar probing type questions. Later the teachers introduced the traditional school type questions so that the children could become accustomed to the style which they would encounter in the future (Nieto, 1992).

Cultural differences in nonverbal signals can lead to misunderstandings that impair communication (Morain, 1986). Eye contact patterns in middle class Euro-pean American groups find speakers establishing contact with their listener for a second or two, then glancing away as they continue to talk; in a few moments they re-establish eye contact to assure themselves that the listener is attentive, then shift their gaze away once more. The listener, meanwhile, keeps an unbroken gaze on the eyes of the speaker, for if the speaker should check back at a time when the listener's eyes are wandering, the communicative rapport would be broken. Few white Americans can describe this pattern, although they practice it a hundred times a day. It exists at an out-of-awareness level. Consequently, when it is violated (by a Puerto Rican student, an African American child, or a student from Asia—whose cultures feel that it is disrespectful to look an authority figure in the eye) a feeling of antagonism is engendered.

Au (1992) reports research which showed that European American counselors in a college setting had difficulty in accurately reading the listening behaviors of African American students. During the counseling sessions, students failed to nod their heads and make accepting noises such as "Um-hmm" at the times when the counselors anticipated them. Instead, they timed their head nods in the way customarily observed in their own culture. Feeling that the students were not concentrating on the advice they were giving them, the frustrated counselors kept on explaining the same point, a situation which irked the students, who felt that they were being "talked down to." The frequency of such miscommunications is far greater than we realize because kinesic cues are often below the level of our awareness.

The American teacher's insistence on "getting to the point" in class discussions is readily understood by mainstream students. Althen (1988) points out, however, that it may be baffling to students from other cultures:

> The "point" is the idea or piece of information that Americans presume is, or should be, at the center of people's thinking, writings, and spoken comments. Speakers and writers are supposed to "make their points clear." ... People from many other cultures have different ideas about the point.

Africans traditionally recount stories that convey the thoughts they have in mind, rather than stating "the point" explicitly. Japanese traditionally speak indirectly, leaving the listener to figure out what the point is.... It is not enough to make a point, according to the typical American notion. A responsible speaker or writer is also expected to prove that the point is true, accurate, or valid. As they grow up, Americans learn ...(that) the most important element of a proof is "the facts."...Americans assume there are "facts" of life, of nature, and of the universe that can be discovered by trained people (usually called "scientists").... "Scientific facts"... are assumed to exist independently of any individual person who studies them or talks about them. This important assumption—that there are facts existing independently of the people who observe them—is not shared throughout the world. (pp. 30-31)

Thus, something as central to the learning process as ways of reasoning may bewilder students from diverse cultures.

It is easy to see that the cultural **function** of *learning* encompasses a host of **forms** which differ markedly from one culture to another. It is crucial that teachers be sensitive and aware, for they must be able to do far more than deliver the old lecture on "Education in Spain" or "A School Day in Germany." They must know the culture-conditioned expectations for learning of the varied students in their own classroom. Since students, regardless of their home culture, are all participants in the culture of the classroom, it can be the starting point for learning about functions and forms of culture, about stereotypes and prejudice, about the absence of shared values, about the tendency to look at C2 with the C1 eye and the faulty assumptions that ensue. Byrnes (1991: 213) suggests that these "processes and strategies for developing cultural awareness are ultimately more important than the details of the product."

QUESTION 5: How can we enable students to make connections between their own culture, the culture of the classroom, and the culture of the target language?

Discussion

A decade ago I jotted into the front page of my grade book a line from an article published in some now-forgotten journal: **"Expect more, teach more, care more."** Each time I rework the syllabus for a class, that six-word exhortation becomes increasingly insistent. Perhaps it could serve as the leit-motif for the final section of this chapter.

Expect more: Recent research with a broad national data base (Oakes, 1986) concluded that white and affluent students generally receive more effective teaching than do students in other groups and that the teaching of minority and poor pupils was largely limited to basic literacy and low-level computational skills. Renyi (1994: 439-40) reminds us that "a basic drill-for-skill education is rather boring. In such classrooms one reads a story for the sole purpose of answering the teacher's questions." Unfortunately, as she points out, a self-fulfilling prophecy takes hold in the pedagogy of poverty. Basic skills are offered; students find them tedious and fail to learn them. Basic skills are offered again and again, in a relentless—and futile—effort to *force* children to learn them. Meanwhile, the humanities are put off indefinitely. The students never get a chance to read real books, understand real history, or grapple with the questions and problems that have intrigued and beguiled humanity for thousands of years.

Fortunately, the foreign language classroom is an intrinsically exciting environment. Here, students can explore a mysterious new system that uses intriguing sounds in curious arrangements to convey messages accessible only to those who know the secrets of the code. Furthermore, there is rich possibility for comradeship with those who share the adventure. All students—whether immigrant, co-culture, or mainstream; whether "honors" or "at risk"—begin their study of the new language at the same point: zero.

Teach more: One important new concept which has bearing on our discussion is the theory of *multiple intelligences*, which challenges teachers to look at cognitive differences among students in a new way (Walters and Gardner, 1986) . Believing that cognitive competence is best described as a *set* of talents, abilities, or mental skills, Gardner expands the list of intelligences to seven: linguistic and logical-mathematical, certainly—the two to which most of our present-day schooling is devoted—but in addition, musical, bodily-kinesthetic, spatial, interpersonal, and intrapersonal intelligences. To illustrate the argument for multiple intelligences, Oddleifson (1994: 448) focuses on the arts:

> These arts-related intelligences are the source of concepts, and concepts are essential for the construction of meaning. Since the arts represent organized forms of perception, we conclude that higher levels of abstract thought—i.e., critical and creative thinking capabilities—are dependent to a significant extent on artistic thinking.... Aesthetic understanding is reached by connecting the intellect with the senses.... The arts provide connections that allow lateral leaps between cognitive domains, which can produce sudden scientific insights.

Designating as *intelligences* certain abilities previously referred to as *talents* or *skills* opens the way for new teaching and evaluation procedures, as well as new opportunities for validating the cognitive strengths of the culturally diverse students in our classroom.   A teacher searching for specific activities to help students grow in their ability to analyze, to evaluate, and to clarify priorities as they engage in authentic language and culture learning activities will find a treasure trove of suggestions in the four appendices at the end of Galloway's (1992) chapter on reading authentic texts.

Care more: Finally, teachers must believe that the individual culture of each child is valuable and capable of adding rich dimensions to the learning experiences of the entire class.   Teachers can find ways to help each student make connections between his/her culture, the culture of the classroom world, and the culture of the target language.   A teacher of German, for instance, can teach students how to objectively compare an aspect of German culture with that of mainstream America.   Discussion gives the students a conceptual framework and the necessary vocabulary to talk about intercultural differences intelligently.   If there are regional differences concerning that aspect in the United States, or variations by co-cultures, students discuss them.   If there are students in the class of international origin, they present the comparable point of culture from their homeland.   Day after day, students gradually acquire the mindset that being different does not necessarily mean being wrong and that problems usually have more than one acceptable solution.   As Walker (1983) reminds us:

What is always needed in the appreciation of art, or life, is the larger perspective. Connections made, or at least attempted, where none existed before; the straining to encompass in one's glance at the varied world the common thread, the unifying theme through immense diversity, a fearlessness of growth, or search...that enlarges the private and the public world (p. 5).

If we do our job well, it is this mindset—openness to the larger perspective, questing for the unifying theme—which goes through the door of the foreign language class, down the hall, and out into life with our students.

Bibliography

Althen, G. 1988. *American Ways: A Guide for Foreigners in the United States.* Yarmouth, ME: Intercultural Press.

Au, K. 1992. *Literacy Instruction in Multicultural Settings.* Fort Worth: Harcourt Brace Jovanovich.

Abrahams, R. 1970. *Positively Black.* Englewood Cliffs, NJ: Prentice-Hall.

Brislin, R. 1993. *Understanding Culture's Influence on Behavior.* New York: Harcourt Brace College Publishers.

Brown, R. 1991. *Schools of Thought: How the Politics of Literacy Shape Thinking in the Classroom.* San Francisco: Jossey-Bass.

Byrnes, H. 1991. "Reflections on the Development of Cross-cultural Communicative Competence in the Foreign Language Classroom," in B. F. Freed, ed., *Foreign Language Acquisition Research and the Classroom.* Lexington, MA: D. C. Heath.

Cheng, L. 1987. *Assessing Asian Language Performance: Guidelines for Evaluating Limited-English-Proficiency Students.* Rockville, MD: Aspen Publishers.

Elkins, R., T. Kalivoda, and G. Morain. 1972. "Teaching Culture through the Audio-motor Unit." *Foreign Language Annals* 6: 61-67.

Galloway, V. 1992. "Toward a Cultural Reading of Authentic Texts." in H. Byrnes, ed., *Languages for a Multicultural World in Transition.* Lincolnwood, IL: National Textbook.

Hale-Benson, J. 1982. *Black Children: Their Roots, Culture and Learning Styles.* Provo, UT: Brigham Young University Press.

Hall, J. and A. Ramirez. 1993. "How a Group of High School Learners of Spanish Perceives the Cultural Identities of Spanish Speakers, English Speakers, and Themselves." *Hispania* 76: 613-20.

Hanvey, R. 1979. "Cross Cultural Awareness." in E. C. Smith and L. F. Luce, eds., *Toward Internationalism: Readings in Cross-Cultural Communication.* Rowley, MA: Newbury House.

Heath, S. 1982. "Questioning at Home and at School: A Comparative Study." in G. Spindler, ed., *Doing the Ethnography of Schooling: Educational Anthropology in Action.* New York: Holt, Rinehart & Winston.

Hernandez, S. and I. Santiago. "Toward a Qualitative Analysis of Teacher Disapproval Behavior," in R. Padilla, ed., *Theory, Technology, and Public Policy on Bilingual Education.* Rosslyn, VA.: National Clearinghouse for Bilingual Education.

Hewett, N. M. 1985. "Reading, Cognitive Style and Culture: A Look at Some Relationships in Second-Language Acquisition," in A. Labarca and L. M. Bailey, eds., *Issues in L2: Theory as Practice/Practice as Theory.* Norwood, NJ: Ablex.

Kluckhohn, F. and F. Strodtbeck. 1961. *Variations in Value Orientations.* Evanston, IL: Row, Peterson.

Kochman, T. 1989. "Black and White Cultural Styles in Pluralistic Perspective," in B. Gifford, ed., *Test Policy and Test Performance: Education, Language, and Culture.* Boston: Kluwer Academic Publishers.

Kochman, T. 1981. *Black and White Styles in Conflict.* Chicago: University of Chicago Press.

Kramsch, C. 1991. "The Order of Discourse in Language Teaching," in B. F. Freed, ed., *Foreign Language Acquisition Research and the Classroom.* Lexington, MA: D. C. Heath.

Lindfors, J. 1989. "The Classroom: A Good Environment for Language Learning," in P. Rigg and V. Allen, eds., *When They Don't All Speak English: Integrating the ESL Student into the Regular Classroom.* Urbana, IL: National Council of Teachers of English.

Morain, G. 1986. "Kinesics Across Cultures." in J. Valdes, ed., *Culture Bound: Bridging the Cultural Gap in Language Teaching.* New York: Cambridge University Press.

Nieto, S. 1992. *Confirming Diversity: The Sociopolitical Context of Multicultural Education.* New York: Longman.

Oakes, J. 1986. "Tracking, Inequality, and the Rhetoric of School Reform: Why Schools Don't Change. *Journal of Education* 168: 61-80.

Oddleifson, E. 1994. "What Do We Want Our Schools To Do?" *Phi Delta Kappan* 75: 446-53.

Ortuno, M. 1991. "Cross-cultural Awareness in the Foreign Language Class: The Kluckhohn Model." *Modern Language Journal* 75: 449-59

Ramirez, M. and A. Castaneda. 1974. *Cultural Democracy, Bicognitive Development and Education.* New York: Academic Press.

Renyi, J. 1994. "The Arts and Humanities in American Education." *Phi Delta Kappan* 75: 438-45.

Robinson, G. 1988. *Crosscultural Understanding.* Hemel Hempstead, Hertfordshire (UK): Prentice Hall International.

Sapir, E. 1951. "The Unconscious Patterning of Behavior in Society," in D. G. Mandelbaum, ed., Selected Writings of Edward Sapir in Language, Culture, and Personality. Berkeley: University of California Press.

Sleeter, C. and C. Grant. 1994. *Making Choices for Multicultural Education: Five Approaches to Race, Class, and Gender.* New York: Macmillan.

Toelken, B. 1979. *The Dynamics of Folklore.* Boston: Houghton Mifflin.

Walker, A. 1983. *In Search of Our Mother's Gardens.* New York: Harcourt Brace Jovanovich.

Walters, J. and H. Gardner. 1986. "The Theory of Multiple Intelligences: Some Issues and Answers," in R. Sternberg and R. Wagner, eds., *Practical Intelligences*. New York: Cambridge University Press.

Witkin, H. 1962. *Psychological Differentiation*. New York: Wiley.

Wong Fillmore, L. 1986. "Research Currents: Equity or Excellence?" *Language Arts* 63: 474-78.

chapter 5

Listening

Eileen W. Glisan

Indiana University of Pennsylvania

QUESTION 1: **What is the role of listening in the proficiency-oriented foreign language curriculum?**

Discussion

Listening plays a central role in all learning in one's native language (Feyten, 1991). Research indicates that we spend more of our time listening (45% or more) than we do in communicating by means of any of the other skills (Rivers, 1975; Rankin, 1930). Coakley and Wolvin (1986) cite studies that support the key role of listening "... in the educational process, in social interactions, and in career success" (p. 36). According to Curtis (1986), not only is listening the primary learning vehicle for college students, but it may also be a more crucial predictor of academic success than one's IQ score.

Several studies done in foreign and second language learning have shown significant relationships between listening ability and overall language proficiency (Winitz and Reeds, 1973; Asher, Kusudo, and de la Torre, 1974; Postovsky, 1981; Asher, 1982; Feyten, 1991). Further, research suggests that a positive transfer occurs from listening to speaking and reading; that is, students who are trained in listening skill also develop speaking and reading skills without specific training in these areas (Nord, 1981).

Historically, the receptive skills of listening and reading have received less attention in language classrooms than have the productive skills of speaking and writing. Methods of teaching foreign languages, such as the Direct Method and the Audiolingual Method, stressed early and ongoing exposure to oral language, but failed to teach students **how** to listen effectively. Over the past several years, the profession has recognized that mere exposure to oral input is not sufficient and that specific strategies for teaching listening are necessary (Joiner, 1986).   Research in language acquisition continues to lend support to classroom instruction that is communicative or proficiency-oriented in nature, i.e., that provides opportunities for students to communicate and interact with one another in the target language (Higgs, 1984; Omaggio Hadley, 1993). Listening skill is paramount in a curriculum that focuses on building communicative ability. As Byrnes (1985) acknowledges, "We have found not merely a complete compatibility, but the indispensability of competence in listening and reading for the communicative classroom" (p. 104). Within the context of a communicative syllabus, Joiner (1986) cites four recent developments in language instruction which have brought about a greater interest in listening comprehension: (1) implementation of comprehension-based approaches, which propose that comprehension is the basic means by which language is internalized, and which advocate a pre-speaking or silent listening period; (2) an increasing emphasis on both listening and reading; (3) development of functional-notional approaches, which focus on listening and speaking geared to the oral communicative needs of students; and (4) the creation of the ACTFL Proficiency Guidelines, which present the listening process within a developmental framework (pp. 45-46).

QUESTION 2:   What factors should teachers consider when planning for listening instruction?

Discussion

Given the current emphasis on proficiency-oriented instruction, there are several important considerations teachers should make when planning for listening instruction:

1) **The listener's background knowledge and prediction strategies and how to activate them.**
Teachers should be sure that students have the background knowledge necessary for listening tasks. The listener must be able to merge the context and the message with already existing background knowledge or "schemata" (Minsky, 1982). Byrnes (1985) warns that meanings are not extracted from messages but rather are brought to the text by the listener in a particular way, based on previous knowledge and experiences. In other words, a text does not necessarily have one meaning which all

listeners must discover; rather, each listener derives a particular meaning based largely on personal background and experiences. Listeners use strategies such as guessing in context, which enable them to predict forthcoming input, facilitating what Oller (1983) calls "activation of correct expectancies" (p. 10). Teachers can facilitate comprehension by preparing students for the listening task through pre-listening stages. Byrnes (1984) suggests that the teacher provide "ethnographic cues" to help students follow the text and predict the content: "... the number of participants, their ages, their personal situations, their likely communicative goals, the physical setting of the interchange, cultural peculiarities that might come into play, special characteristics of the text type ..." (p. 326). The use of advance organizers (comprehension aids presented prior to the listening task) was first advocated by Ausubel (1961) when he suggested that the retention of unfamiliar but meaningful material could be enhanced by the advance introduction of relevant concepts. Advance organizers often take the form of pictures, verbal descriptions, key vocabulary, prequestioning techniques, or cultural background cues. Findings from L1 and L2 research have supported the use of advance organizers to enhance listening comprehension of oral texts (Bransford and Johnson, 1972; Mueller, 1980) and of videos (Herron, 1994).

2) The listener's purpose for listening.

Listening tasks should reflect real listening purposes. Further, the purpose for listening to the task will determine the type of strategies used. Wolvin and Coakley (1985) have developed a taxonomy of listening functions that reflect the listener's purpose: **discriminative, comprehensive, therapeutic** (or empathic), **critical**, or **appreciative**. In a similar vein, Lund (1990) approaches the notion of listening purpose in terms of "listener function," defined as "the aspects of the message the listener attempts to process" (p. 107). He has developed a framework for teaching listening comprehension using listener function (purpose) and listener response. Possible functions or purposes for listening include: identification, orientation, main idea comprehension, detail comprehension, full comprehension, and replication. Listener responses include tasks such as doing, choosing, transferring, answering, condensing, extending, duplicating, modeling, and conversing. Teachers can use this taxonomy to design listening instruction so that the full range of listening functions is practiced. According to Lund (1990), "... growth in proficiency can be seen as progressing through the functions, e.g., learning to do new functions with old texts and to do old functions with new topics or more difficult texts" (p. 112). As is the case with the proficiency guidelines for listening, this taxonomy does not imply a linear progression of activities, but rather a cyclical, repetitive one, in which the listener may work on several functions at once.

3) The listening input: text type, text length, level of difficulty.
An important question in planning for listening instruction is, "What kind of target language input will best help students develop their listening skill?" Some research has indicated that beginning- and intermediate-level students benefit from "teacher talk" or "caretaker speech," which consists of simplified syntax, slower articulation, rephrasing and repetition, use of familiar vocabulary and use of nonverbal aids such as gestures to facilitate comprehension (Krashen, Terrell, Ehrman, and Herzog, 1984). However, extreme care must be taken not to simplify the language and slow it down to a degree that makes it unnatural.

Krashen's (1982) work in the area of input processing has played a key role in sparking discussion and debate concerning the nature of oral input and its effect on language acquisition. In his Input Hypothesis, Krashen (1982) maintains that acquisition in the classroom occurs when language is presented under certain conditions: when learners attend to comprehensible input that is interesting, a little beyond their current level of competence, **not** grammatically sequenced, and provided in an environment where students are "off the defensive" (p. 127). Krashen's theories are compatible with several current-day comprehension-based methodologies such as the Natural Method and the Total Physical Response Method, in which students are exposed to extensive amounts of language input (made comprehensible by gestures, pictures, etc.), develop comprehension skills, and then progress gradually to productive use. Although Krashen's theory has prompted the profession to examine the key role of target language input, much research remains to be done in order to shed light on the exact nature of comprehensible input.

As to what kind of texts are conducive to developing listening comprehension skills, Oller (1983) maintains that certain types of texts are easier to internalize that others. According to Oller's (1983) Episode Hypothesis, "text (i.e., discourse in any form) will be easier to reproduce, understand, and recall, to the extent that it is motivated and structured episodically" (p. 12). "Episodic organization" refers to how logically organized and interesting a text is. A text that has motivation has an apparent purpose, captures the interest of the listener, and features a story-type conflict. A text that is logically sequenced is structured like a good story and connects with our meaningful experiences of the world. In his discussion on implications of the Episode Hypothesis for language teaching, Oller (1983) states that "...perhaps second language teaching would be more successful if it incorporated principles of good story writing along with the benefits of sound linguistic analysis" (p. 12).

Much discussion in the area of input has centered on the use of authentic materials in the classroom. Villegas Rogers and Medley (1988) have defined authentic materials as "... language samples—both oral and written—that reflect a naturalness of form, and an appropriateness of cultural and situational context that would be found in the language used by native speakers" (p. 468). Geddes and White (1978) identify two types of authentic texts: (1) **unmodified** authentic discourse, which is prepared by native speakers for native speakers of the language; and (2) **simulated** authentic discourse, which is language prepared for instructional purposes, but which is likely to occur in target language communication. Use of authentic materials offers students the opportunity to hear real language with a purpose and to explore real culture that is inherent in the texts. Some researchers have expressed concern that the use of unmodified authentic texts may cause the listener to experience difficulty and frustration (Dunkel, 1986; Ur, 1984). However, more recent studies present convincing evidence to support the use of these materials, even in early levels of instruction. In Bacon's (1992a) study, beginning-level Spanish students who listened to authentic discourse demonstrated a range of comprehension skill, with some students progressing to the point of learning new information or new vocabulary, or of evaluating the content of the texts. These results led Bacon to conclude that authentic, unedited discourse has a place in the beginning-level curriculum. Similarly, in Herron and Seay's (1991) experiment, intermediate-level French students who listened to unedited authentic radio segments in place of other communicative oral activities and grammar practice demonstrated significantly greater listening comprehension than did their counterparts who did not listen to the segments.

One avenue through which the profession has implemented simulated authentic discourse is **semiscripting** (Geddes and White, 1978). Semiscripting is done by giving native speakers a semiscript—an outline or notes—that describes a conversation or situation to be created. The native speakers spontaneously create the conversation based on the outline, which may describe key vocabulary and structures to be used or merely the content to be included. The discourse created is then taped onto audiotapes or videotapes for classroom use. Semiscripted discourse provides a compromise between unmodified authentic discourse and scripted textbook dialogues. Since they are spontaneous in nature and produced by native speakers, semiscripted conversations provide authentic-like input for students which may be less threatening than purely authentic discourse. The profession still needs further study regarding the effectiveness of authentic and semiscripted texts, their appropriateness at various levels of instruction, and specific techniques for presenting and exploiting them.

Current research indicates that the appropriateness of a text should be judged in conjunction with tasks required of listeners and not exclusively on the basis of the difficulty of the text itself (Byrnes, 1985; Joiner, 1986; Lund, 1990). For example, students who are given an authentic advertisement announcing a clothing sale might be asked to identify only the numbers they hear or the items of clothing that are on sale; later on, students might hear the ad again and be asked to identify other details and discuss them. Students should not be expected to understand **every** detail and word with the first listening, but should be provided opportunities to understand more and more with additional passes through the text. Further, students should be given guidance as they listen. Eykyn's (1992) study examined the effects of four types of listening guides provided to students as they heard authentic texts in French: multiple choice guide; vocabulary list guide; picture guide; and the who-, what-, where-, why-guide. The results of this study indicated that the multiple choice guide facilitated listening comprehension significantly better than did the other three guides. The vocabulary guide was second in effectiveness, the picture guide was third, and the wh-question guide was last (Eykyn, 1992). Future research must continue to examine the types of listening assistance that most effectively facilitate comprehension.

Little, if any, research has examined the effect of text length on listening comprehension. Studies done in reading comprehension have indicated that longer texts may actually be easier for students to comprehend because they are more cohesive and provide more context. Students who attend to shorter texts may be more likely to use word-for-word processing strategies since the demand on memory allows for more attention to details. Shrum and Glisan (1994) suggest that this may also be the case in listening, although this claim merits corroboration through further research.

4)   Treatment of new structures and vocabulary.

Research in the area of how to deal with new grammatical structures and vocabulary words in listening is minimal. Meyer (1984) suggests an activity known as **lexicon recovery** to teach students "... to recover unknown words by continuing to listen and chaining the unknown items to familiar items in the passage" (p. 344). For example, students might be asked to find all references to a specific unfamiliar word in the oral text, listen to find out if the word refers to a person, place, or thing, and guess the meaning of the word using the contextual clues. In a post-listening activity, students might read a transcript of the text and identify all the words that helped them understand the meaning of the word (Joiner, 1986).

Shrum and Glisan (1994) apply research findings involving treatment of new vocabulary in reading to the listening process. Pre- and post-listening discussion might be used to present new vocabulary and link it to listeners' background knowledge (Grellet, 1981; Nuttall, 1982). As suggested by Swaffar, Arens, and Byrnes (1991) in reading skill development, teachers might provide in-class vocabulary practice for listening that enables students to find words that relate to similar semantic categories, identify affixes and parts of speech, and identify how the same words are redefined by different contexts. Phillips' (1984) "decoding" stage in reading might also be adapted for use in listening instruction so that students might be able "... to expand vocabulary, to see how the cohesive elements of the discourse operate ..." (p. 292). For example, students might identify the effect of sentence connectors, a particular tense, a category of pronouns, or word order on meaning in the discourse heard. These suggestions are clearly tentative ones that could be the basis for future research.

QUESTION 3: Some language learners seem to acquire listening skill very easily, while others experience a great deal of difficulty. What factors are involved in listening to and understanding foreign language speech? What types of strategies do students use as they listen? Are certain comprehension strategies more effective than others?

Discussion

Since the research specific to second-language listening is scant at best, a great deal of the theory and applications of how language learners attend to target language input has been gleaned from studies of reading and first language listening (Joiner, 1986; Lund, 1990). [For a comprehensive review of first- and second-language listening and reading, see Wing, 1986.] We know that listening is an active process that involves an interplay between various types of knowledge. Scarcella and Oxford (1992) have described the listening process in terms of Canale and Swain's (1980) model of communicative competence. According to this model, listeners use four types of competencies as they process an oral message:

1) **grammatical competence:** knowledge of morphology, syntax, and vocabulary;

2) **sociolinguistic competence:** knowledge of what is expected socially and culturally by native speakers of the target language;

3) **discourse competence:** the ability to use cohesion devices such as pronouns, conjunctions, and transitional phrases to link meaning across sentences, as well as the ability to recognize how coherence is used to maintain the unity of the message;

4) **strategic competence:** the ability to use a number of guessing strategies to compensate for missing knowledge (Canale and Swain, 1980).

Listeners rely on the types of knowledge described above as they perform a variety of comprehension tasks. The manner in which listeners approach the task at hand seems to depend on their ability to use a variety of comprehension strategies, as well as on their individual learning styles. According to Anderson (1985), the choice of listeners' strategies depends on the **phase** of the listening task. During the **perceptual** phase, listeners store the sounds they hear in echoic memory and use contextual information to anticipate what they will hear. In other words, they begin to process the sounds for meaning almost immediately and use the contextual information to predict what they will hear next. In the **parsing** phase, listeners store meaningful chunks of information in short-term memory and begin to construct meaning. It is in this stage that information is reorganized into meaningful units that will be kept in short-term memory. Finally, during the **utilization** phase, listeners use prior knowledge from long-term memory to connect the oral message with information they already have; this stored information consists of concepts that were learned previously and interrelated with new ones (Anderson, 1985). Evidence suggests that listeners do not experience these phases in a linear fashion, but that the individual listening strategies interrelate and repeat the phases (O'Malley, Chamot, and Küpper, 1989).

Oxford (1990b) has classified six general types of language learning strategies often used by students in language tasks, such as listening, in order to facilitate their own learning:

1) **planning/evaluating** (metacognitive) **strategies**, such as paying attention, consciously searching for practice opportunities, planning for language tasks, self-evaluating one's progress, and monitoring errors;

2) **emotional/motivational** (affective) **strategies**, such as anxiety reduction, self-encouragement, and self-reward;

3) **social strategies**, such as asking questions, cooperating with native speakers of the language, and becoming culturally aware;

4) **memory strategies**, such as grouping, imagery, rhyming, and structured reviewing;

5) **cognitive strategies**, such as reasoning, analyzing, summarizing, and general practicing;

6) **compensation strategies** (to compensate for limited knowledge), such as guessing meanings from the context in reading and listening, and using synonyms and gestures to convey meaning when the precise expression is not known. [See also Scarcella and Oxford, 1992.]

Some of the strategies described above involve **top-down processing**, in which the listener derives meaning by first attending to whole chunks of meaningful language, and then by using contextual clues and personal background knowledge to piece together meaning. Other strategies, such as analyzing, reflect **bottom-up processing**, in which the listener builds meaning sequentially, combining sounds or letters to form words, then combining words to form phrases, clauses, and sentences of the text (Goodman, 1967). The current view of the listening process is that it involves both bottom-up and top-down processing.

There are few studies in foreign language learning that examine strategy use by listeners. However, the studies that have been completed in this area have attempted to distinguish between effective and ineffective listening strategies. Chamot and colleagues (1987) found that more effective learners used top-down strategies, such as anticipating and predicting from background knowledge. Relevant to their research, therefore, good listeners used previously learned information to help them construct meaning, periodically monitored or checked their level of comprehension, and used the purpose for listening to guide their strategy use. In their investigations of listener strategies, Bacon (1992b) and Murphy (1987) both concluded that the most successful listeners were those who used a wider variety of strategies. Bacon's (1992b) study of listening strategies used by nonproficient learners of Spanish as they listened to authentic oral Spanish revealed trends in many strategy categories. More successful listeners, for example, used a greater number and range of strategies, effectively used background knowledge, could summarize and add detail, and were able to refocus when attention was lost. In comparison, less successful listeners tended to use only one or two strategies, were overdependent on background knowledge, were unable to summarize, were satisfied with comprehending few details, and had difficulty refocusing when attention was lost (Bacon, 1992b: 327). According to Bacon (1992b), "More successful listeners seemed to be flexible, moving from bottom-up to top-down strategies as they progressed from the perceptual to the parsing phases" (p. 331). One of the interesting findings in Bacon's (1992b) study was that listeners did not use all of the comprehension strategies that they normally use in their native language. Bacon's (1992b) insights, gained from her experiment, led her to conclude that if students are aware of the variety of listening strategies at their disposal, they can more effectively select, use, and adapt those that are of greatest assistance to them.

The degree to which listeners use top-down or bottom-up strategies may be determined to a certain extent by their individual learning styles. Scarcella and Oxford (1992) and Oxford (1990a) describe five components of learning styles:

1) **analytic-global**: the difference between a detail-oriented individual and a holistic one;

2) **sensory preferences**: the physical, perceptual avenues for learning, such as visual, auditory, and hands-on;

3) **intuitive/random** and **sensory/sequential learning**: the type of organization students prefer in the presentation of material, abstract and global vs. step-by-step, ordered;

4) **orientation to closure**: the degree to which students need to reach conclusions and can tolerate ambiguity; and

5) **competition-cooperation**: the degree to which learners benefit from competing against or cooperating with others.

According to Byrnes (1985), the learner who seems to be most successful in comprehension tasks is the one who is more flexible and willing to tolerate a certain amount of ambiguity. It is clear, however, that much more research in second language listening is needed in order to further corroborate these preliminary findings concerning the relationship between listening skill and learning strategies/cognitive styles.

QUESTION 4: How can listening be taught without compromising time needed for the other areas? What instructional techniques best develop listening proficiency?

Discussion

One format for listening activities is suggested by Scarcella and Oxford's (1992) "Tapestry Approach," which treats listening as an important part of the communicative process whereby students learn to receive and share meaning. In this type of approach, students are actively involved in listening tasks and use the information to communicate with one another. The Tapestry Approach has the following features:

& Students collaborate on authentic listening tasks (jigsaw, group activities, etc.).

& Listening topics are student-generated to a great extent.

  ▟   Students are encouraged to guess while listening and are given strategies to do so; they also learn other key strategies for listening.

  ▟   Teachers recognize that listening is easier for auditory students than for students with a visual or hands-on style, and they routinely provide help (visuals, realia) for listeners who need it. (Scarcella and Oxford, 1992: 140)

The interactive nature of the Tapestry Approach stands in sharp contrast to traditional approaches for teaching listening, such as: students work alone with tapes; listening topics are teacher-controlled; students do not receive help in guessing while listening; and teachers do not pay attention to differences in listening ability based on learning styles (Scarcella and Oxford, 1992: 140).

The components of the Tapestry Approach might be used with the types of listening comprehension activities suggested by Omaggio Hadley (1993) for learners at different levels of language proficiency. [See Appendix A for a list of sample tasks according to Novice/Intermediate and Advanced/Superior levels of the ACTFL Proficiency Guidelines.] As Omaggio Hadley (1993) indicates, several strategies listed at the lower two levels provide extralinguistic support, such as visuals and physical activity, for students whose listening abilities are weaker, while the tasks at the higher levels elicit more detailed comprehension.

One of the reasons that listening comprehension has not received sufficient attention in language teaching is that it has been treated as a separate skill in many of the teaching strategies that have been suggested. The research does not abound with ideas for how to integrate listening within a given chapter or unit and with the other skills. If listening is to take its prominent place in a proficiency-oriented curriculum, it must be combined with practice of the other skills. Shrum and Glisan (1994) have developed a model for teaching interactive listening and reading which guides students through the text, engages them in interaction with the text, helps them to develop comprehension strategies, and improves their comprehension. As outlined in Appendix B, the model is interactive and procedural, guiding learners as they interact with the text by using both bottom-up and top-down processes; it is also integrative, since it provides opportunities for students to combine listening, speaking, reading, and writing as they derive meaning from the text, recreate the text, and react to the text in a personal way. This framework is based on the Interactive Model for Reading suggested by Eskey (1986), the Procedural Model for Integrative Reading proposed by Swaffar, Arens, and Byrnes (1991), and several aspects of Phillips' (1984) Classroom Plan for Developing Reading Comprehension. Shrum and Glisan (1994) suggest that the extent to which each stage in the model is completed in its entirety will depend on the nature of the text and listening task as well as on the instructional objectives.

An important issue that teachers continue to confront when teaching listening is how much of the native versus target language to use in exploring oral texts. Some evidence suggests that occasional use of the native language to check for comprehension may be beneficial, since it eliminates the possibility of confusing comprehension with production of the target language (Swaffar, Arens, and Byrnes, 1991; Lee, 1986). It may be useful at times to conduct the pre-listening activities in the native language, especially if students need new background information prior to the listening task. The decision to use either the native or target language must clearly be made by the individual teacher while considering the level of students' proficiency and the task to be done.

Another avenue for placing listening at the center of language teaching is with whole language teaching. Recent studies have identified the benefits of "whole language instruction," in which students acquire language by hearing or reading authentic, whole texts (usually literary readings), while learning to process meaning within context (Adair-Hauck, Donato, and Cumo, 1994). Shrum and Glisan (1994) describe a strategy for contextualizing language instruction using a top-down, whole language approach that builds upon listening skill: within a given thematic unit, the teacher presents an authentic oral text that contains examples of the content, structures, and vocabulary to be taught and practiced in context. Students are guided through the text and perform a series of tasks such as identifying main ideas and specific details, discussing and recreating the text, reading related printed material, and writing compositions dealing with the same theme.

QUESTION 5: How should listening comprehension be assessed?

Discussion

If listening skill is to be a central part of a communicative curriculum, then it must also be assessed. Frequently, tests that are labeled as "listening" assess anything but aural comprehension: memory recall, reading comprehension, vocabulary recognition, speaking ability (Anderson, 1972; Dunkel, Henning, and Chaudron, 1993). Coakley and Wolvin (1986) suggest that listening tests

❧   should not be dependent on written language;

❧   should account for the interactive nature of communication;

❧   should elicit listening skill from the student;

  should provide for a wide range of response options; and

  should allow for teacher, self, and peer observation.

In an attempt to integrate not only teaching but testing, Shrum and Glisan (1994) adapted Swaffar, Arens, and Brynes' Interactive Model for Testing Reading (1991) for use with listening. Within the framework of a real context, the model tests students on their listening ability; grammatical, lexical, and cultural knowledge; skill in interacting with the oral text; and productive skills. In the model, students perform the following tasks:

1) Listen to an authentic oral text.

2) Identify main ideas by focusing on content or text schema.
   Instructions: Identify and write down key words from the text which provide the following information about the main idea of the text:
   who:_____ what: _____
   when:_____ where: _____
   Using these words, write a sentence expressing the main idea of the text.

3) Identify details (vocabulary development).
   Instructions: Find synonyms or references from the text for the following words:

4) Use the grammatical structures in the text to further explore text ideas.
   Instructions: In the story/conversation, the events and their timing are of major importance. Write two sentences about major events in the story. Use past tenses.

5) Students develop their points of view.
   Instructions: What do you think would have happened if the story/conversation had continued? Write (or describe orally) a 3-5 sentence description of another ending to the story/conversation. (This section could also engage students in attention to particular cultural points.)
   (Adapted from Shrum & Glisan, 1994, and Swaffar, Arens, and Byrnes, 1991)

QUESTION 6: How can video and computer technology best be used to support listening instruction?

Discussion

The use of technology as a valuable aid in language instruction has been the topic of an increasing number of studies (Joiner, 1990; Dunkel, 1991; Garza, 1991; Chun and Brandl, 1992; among others). Garrett (1991) has provided a comprehensive review of trends and issues in technology for language learning. Although a detailed review and analysis of technology is beyond the limited scope of this chapter, a brief discussion will follow that summarizes key technological trends as they pertain to the teaching of listening comprehension. [See Pusack and Otto, this volume, for applications of technology to language teaching and learning.]

Many school districts are now equipped with VCRs and television monitors, which enable the world of video to be brought into the classroom. Video can be presented by means of a videocassette or videodisc and a playback machine. The videodisc is advantageous, since it allows the user to find specific frames quickly, and can accommodate connection of a computer to the videodisc player. There has been a great deal of discussion regarding the use of the **videotext**, or a contextualized segment of video that presents an authentic piece of language. Altman (1989) stresses the golden rule of video pedagogy: "Don't expect—or even seek—full comprehension" (p. 42). He maintains that effective video instruction helps students to "...break down the spoken chain into appropriate chunks.... At the same time, it does not ask them to understand what they are not yet prepared to understand" (Altman, 1989: 42). Teachers should keep in mind the following points as they select video materials:

- Identify the function you expect the program to perform.
- Choose short video segments.
- View the program in its entirety before presenting it to students.
- Manipulate the video in order to make it more understandable.
   (Altman, 1989)

Joiner (1990) has created an evaluation form which teachers can use as they evaluate the potential effectiveness of a videotext. That the proper selection of video materials is critical to student comprehension was verified in Rubin's (1990) study using Spanish video with second-year, second-semester high school students of Spanish. In her experiment, students experienced greater success in comprehension when they watched video which served as a "haven for learning" (Bransford, Sherwood, Kinzer, and Hasselbring, 1985). Video passages with this characteristic connect meaningfully to students' background knowledge and experiences and feature actions which provide clues to what is being said (Rubin, 1990). Rubin (1990) also found that students who received training in how to use the strategy of paying attention to the story line while watching a video outperformed students who were not taught such a strategy. Therefore, appropriate selection of video materials and strategy training may be key variables in the degree of success students experience when given a video task.

With the combination of image and sound in authentic contexts, video provides many different options for combining the two modalities. Altman (1989) suggests strategies such as the following:

- Present image and sound together to reinforce vocabulary and cultural aspects; oral discussion might follow.

- Show the image alone to allow students to focus on the cultural elements.

- Play the sound and image together, engage students in discussion, and then play only the sound without the image to sharpen comprehension skills.

- In advanced classes, play the sound alone first, asking students to guess the events that might be happening in the image.

- Play the sound alone first, then the image alone, asking students to narrate the events happening on the screen.

Just as in the case of audiotapes, students require preparation for video viewing by means of a pre-listening/pre-viewing stage that helps them have success in comprehension. Joiner (1990) suggests listening/viewing tasks such as: **skills-oriented**: open-ended questions, role-play, brainstorming, debate, discussion, note-taking, summaries, continuations; **culture-oriented**: noticing, identifying, comparing, contrasting with other cultures, imitation, role-play; **script-oriented**: finding examples of redundancy, identifying words/phrases used to express emotion, to persuade, etc., rewrite portions of the script, fill-in words omitted from script. Expansion activities proposed by Joiner (1990) include playing games, building or making something, reading related material, and creating an audio or video broadcast. Viewing guides that accompany the video or are created by the teacher are effective as advance organizers in preparing students to watch the video and in facilitating comprehension as they view the segment. [See Lonergan, 1984 for sample pre- and post-viewing guides.]

Clearly, much investigation remains to be done in examining the effects of currently available technological aids on listening pedagogy. A growing body of research is confirming the benefits of technology use in second/foreign language instruction (Secules, Herron, and Tomasello, 1992; Herron and Hanley, 1992; Beauvois, 1992).

However, the profession awaits further study of the various technological advances to help teachers understand how these innovations can serve the goals of their language programs in a cost-effective manner.

> **Note**: Government agencies and radio stations are a good source of free or inexpensive materials and taped segments. For example: French: Radio-Canada International, Montreal, Canada H3CA8; German: German Information Center, 950 Third Ave., NY 10022; Spanish: U.S. Department of Agriculture, Hispanic Information Service, Office of Governmental and Public Affairs, Washington, D.C. 20250.

Bibliography

Adair-Hauck, B., R. Donato, and P. Cumo. 1994. "Using a Whole Language Approach to Teach Grammar," in J. L. Shrum and E. W. Glisan, *Teacher's Handbook: Contextualized Language Instruction*. Boston: Heinle and Heinle.

Altman, R. 1989. *The Video Connection*. Boston: Houghton Mifflin.

Anderson, R. C. 1972. "How to Construct Achievement Tests to Assess Comprehension." *Review of Educational Research*, 42: 145-70.

Anderson, J. R. 1985. *Cognitive Psychology and Its Implications*. New York: Freeman.

Asher, J. J. 1982. *Learning Another Language through Actions: The Complete Teacher's Guide*. Los Gatos, CA: Sky Oaks Productions.

Asher, J. J., J. Kusudo, and R. de la Torre. 1974. "Learning a Second Language through Commands: The Second Field Test." *The Modern Language Journal* 58: 24-32.

Ausubel, D. 1961. "The Use of Advance Organizers in the Learning and Retention of Meaningful Verbal Material." *Journal of Educational Psychology* 51: 266-74.

Bacon, S. M. 1992a. "Authentic Listening in Spanish: How Learners Adjust Their Strategies to the Difficulty of the Input. *Hispania* 75: 398-412.

Bacon, S. M. 1992b. "Phases of Listening to Authentic Input in Spanish: A Descriptive Study." *Foreign Language Annals* 25: 317-24.

Beauvois, M. H. 1992. "Computer-assisted Classroom Discussion in the Foreign Language Classroom: Conversation in Slow Motion." *Foreign Language Annals* 25: 455-64.

Bransford, J. D. and M. K. Johnson. 1972. "Contextual Prerequisites for Understanding: Some Investigations of Comprehension and Recall." *Journal of Verbal Learning and Verbal Behavior* 11: 717-26.

Bransford, J. D., R. D. Sherwood, C. K. Kinzer, and T. S. Hasselbring. 1985. *Havens for Learning: Toward a Framework for Developing Effective Uses of Technology.* Nashville: George Peabody College for Teachers.

Byrnes, H. 1985. "Teaching toward Proficiency: The Receptive Skills," in A. C. Omaggio, ed., *Proficiency, Curriculum, Articulation: The Ties that Bind.* Middlebury, VT: Northeast Conference.

Byrnes, H. 1984. "The Role of Listening Comprehension: A Theoretical Base. *Foreign Language Annals* 17: 317-34.

Canale, M. 1984. "Considerations in the Testing of Reading and Listening Proficiency." *Foreign Language Annals* 17: 349-50.

Canale, M., and M. Swain. 1980. "Theoretical Bases of Communicative Approaches to Second Language Teaching and Testing." *Applied Linguistics* 1: 1-47.

Chamot, A. U., J. M. O'Malley, L. Küpper, and M. V. Impink-Hernández. 1987. *A Study of Learning Strategies in Foreign Language Instruction: First Year Report.* Roslyn, VA: InterAmerica Research Associates.

Chun, D. M., and K. K. Brandl. 1992. "Beyond Form-based Drill and Practice: Meaning-enhanced CALL on the Macintosh." *Foreign Language Annals* 25: 255-67.

Coakley, C. G., and A. D. Wolvin. 1986. "Listening in the Native Language," in B.H. Wing, ed., *Listening, Reading, Writing: Analysis and Application.* Middlebury, VT: Northeast Conference.

Curtis, D. 1986. "College Survival Skills: The Importance of Listening Skills." Paper delivered at Be Here Now Conference, College Survival Inc., San Francisco.

Dunkel, P. A. 1991. *Computer-assisted Language Learning and Testing: Research Issues and Practice.* New York: Newbury House.

Dunkel, P. A. 1986. "Developing Listening Fluency in L2: Theoretical Principles and Pedagogical Considerations. *Modern Language Journal* 70: 99-106.

Dunkel, P., G. Henning, and C. Chaudron. 1993. "The Assessment of an L2 Listening Comprehension Construct: A Tentative Model for Test Specification and Development." *Modern Language Journal* 77: 180-91.

Eskey, D. E. 1986. "Theoretical Foundations." In F. Dubin, D. E. Eskey, and W. Grabe, eds., *Teaching Second Language Reading for Academic Purposes.* Reading, MA: Addison-Wesley.

Eykyn, L. B. 1992. "The Effects of Listening Guides on the Comprehension of Authentic Texts by Novice Learners of French as a Second Language." Doctoral dissertation, University of South Carolina.

Feyten. C. M. 1991. "The Power of Listening Ability: An Overlooked Dimension in Language Acquisition." *Modern Language Journal* 75: 173-80.

Garrett, N. 1991. "Technology in the Service of Language Learning: Trends and Issues." *Modern Language Journal* 75: 74-101.

Garza, T. J. 1991. "Evaluating the Use of Captioned Video Material in Advanced Foreign Language Learning." *Foreign Language Annals* 24: 239-58.

Geddes, M., and R. White. 1978. "The Use of Semi-scripted Simulated Authentic Speech in Listening Comprehension." *Audiovisual Language Journal* 16: 137-45.

Goodman, K. S. 1967. "Reading: A Psycholinguistic Guessing Game. *Journal of the Reading Specialist* 6: 126-35.

Grellet, F. 1981. *Developing Reading Skills. A Practical Guide to Reading Comprehension Exercises.* Cambridge: Cambridge University Press.

Hendrickson, J. M. 1992. "Creating Listening and Speaking Prochievement Tests." *Hispania* 75: 1326-31.

Herron, C. A. 1994. "An Investigation of the Effectiveness of Using an Advance Organizer to Introduce Video in the FL Classroom." *Modern Language Journal* 78: 190-98.

Herron, C. A., and J. Hanley. 1992. "Using Video to Introduce Children to a Foreign Culture." *Foreign Language Annals* 25: 419-26.

Herron, C. A., and I. Seay. 1991. "The Effect of Authentic Oral Texts on Student Listening Comprehension in the Foreign Language Classroom." *Foreign Language Annnals* 24: 487-95.

Higgs, T. V., ed. 1984. *Teaching for Proficiency, the Organizing Principle.* Lincolnwood, IL: National Textbook.

Joiner, E. G. 1991. "Teaching Listening: Ends and Means," in J. E. Alatis, ed., *Georgetown University Round Table on Languages and Linguistics.* Washington, DC: Georgetown University Press.

Joiner, E. G. 1990. "Choosing and Using Videotext." *Foreign Language Annals* 23: 53-64.

Joiner, E.G. 1986. "Listening in the Foreign Language," in B. H. Wing, ed., *Listening, Reading, and Writing: Analysis and Application.* Middlebury, VT: Northeast Conference.

Krashen, S. D. 1982. *Principles and Practice in Second Language Acquisition.* New York: Pergamon.

Krashen, S. D., T. D. Terrell, M. E. Ehrman, and M. A. Herzog. 1984. "A Theoretical Basis for Teaching the Receptive Skills." *Foreign Language Annals* 17: 261-75.

Lee, J. F. 1987. "Comprehending the Spanish Subjunctive: An Information Processing Perspective." *Modern Language Journal* 71: 51-57.

Lee, J. F. 1986. "On the Use of the Recall Task to Measure L2 Reading Comprehension." *Studies in Second Language Acquisition* 8: 83-93.

Lonergan, J. 1984. *Using Video in Language Teaching.* Cambridge: Cambridge University Press.

Lund, R. J. 1990. "A Taxonomy for Teaching Second Language Listening." *Foreign Language Annals* 23: 105-15.

Meyer, R. 1984. "Listen My Children, and You Shall Hear..." *Foreign Language Annals* 17: 343-44.

Mueller, G. A. 1980. "Visual Contextual Clues and Listening Comprehension: An Experiment." *Modern Language Journal* 64: 335-40.

Minsky, M. 1982. "A Framework for Representing Knowledge," in J. Haugeland, ed., *Mind design.* Cambridge, MA: MIT Press.

Murphy, J. M. 1987. "The Listening Strategies of English as a Second Language College Students." *Research and Teaching in Developmental Education* 4: 27-46.

Nord, J. R. 1981. "Three Steps Leading to Listening Fluency: A Beginning," in H. Winitz, ed., *The Comprehension Approach to Foreign Language Instruction.* Rowley, MA: Newbury House.

Nuttal, C. 1982. *Teaching Reading Skills in a Foreign Language.* Practical Language Series no. 9. London: Heinemann.

Oller, J. W. 1983. "Some Working Ideas for Language Teaching," in J. W. Oller and P. A. Richard-Amato, eds., *Methods That Work.* Rowley, MA: Newbury House.

O'Malley, J. M., A. U. Chamot, and L. Küpper. 1989. "Listening Comprehension in Second Language Acquisition. *Applied Linguistics* 10: 418-37.

Omaggio Hadley, A. 1993. *Teaching Language in Context: Proficiency-Oriented Instruction,* 2nd ed. Boston: Heinle and Heinle.

Oxford, R. L. 1990a. "Language Learning Strategies and Beyond: A Look at Strategies in the Context of Styles," in S. Magnan, ed., *Shifting the Instructional Focus to the Learner.* Middlebury, VT: Northeast Conference.

Oxford, R. L. 1990b. *Language Learning Strategies: What Every Teacher Should Know.* New York: Newbury House/Harper and Row..

Phillips, J. K. 1984. "Practical Implications of Recent Research in Reading." *Foreign Language Annals* 17: 285-96.

Postovsky, V. A. 1981. "The Priority of Aural Comprehension in the Language Acquisition Process," in H. Winitz, ed., *The Comprehension Approach to Foreign Language Instruction.* Rowley, MA: Newbury House.

Rankin, P. T. 1930. "Listening Ability: Its Importance, Measurement, and Development." *Chicago Schools Journal,* January 1930: 147-79.

Richards, J. C. 1983. "Listening Comprehension: Approach, Design, Procedure." *TESOL Quarterly* 17: 219-40.

Rivers, W. M. 1975. *A Practical Guide to the Teaching of French.* Oxford: Oxford University Press.

Rubin, J. 1990. "Improving Foreign Language Listening Comprehension," in J. E. Alatis, ed., *Georgetown University Round Table on Languages and Linguistics.* Washington, D.C.: Georgetown University Press.

Scarcella, R. C., and R. L. Oxford. 1992. *The Tapestry of Language Learning.* Boston: Heinle and Heinle.

Secules, T., C. Herron, and M. Tomasello. 1992. "The Effect of Video Context on Foreign Language Learning." *Modern Language Journal* 76: 480-90.

Shrum, J. L., and E. W. Glisan. 1994. *Teacher's Handbook: Contextualized Language Instruction.* Boston: Heinle and Heinle.

Swaffar, J., K. Arens, and H. Byrnes. 1991. *Reading for Meaning.* Englewood Cliffs, NJ: Prentice-Hall.

Ur, P. 1984. *Teaching listening comprehension.* New York: Cambridge University Press.

Villegas Rogers, C., and F. W. Medley, Jr. 1988. "Language with a Purpose: Using Authentic Materials in the Foreign Language Classroom." *Foreign Language Annals* 21: 467-78.

Wing, B. H., ed. 1986. *Listening, Reading, Writing: Analysis and Application.* Middlebury, VT: Northeast Conference.

Winitz, H., and J. Reeds. 1973. "Rapid Acquisition of a Foreign Language by the Avoidance of Speaking." *International Review of Applied Linguistics* 11: 295-317.

Wolvin, A. D., and C. G. Coakley. 1985. *Listening.* 2nd. ed. Dubuque, IA: William C. Brown.

Appendix A

Suggested Tasks for Building Listening Proficiency

Novice/Intermediate
Prelistening activities
Listening for the gist
Listening with visuals
Graphic fill-ins
Matching descriptions to pictures
Dictation and variations (familiar content, simple structures)
Clue searching (listening for cues to meaning, such as key words, syntactic
    features, actor/action/object, etc.)
Distinguishing registers (formal/informal style)
Kinesics/Physical response
Recursive listening (multiple sequenced tasks)
Inferential listening (drawing inferences not presented overtly in the text)
Paraphrase in native language
Completion of native language summary
Comprehension checks (various formats)
Remembering responses of others

Advanced/Superior
Dictation and variations (may include unfamiliar content, more complex structures)
Completing target language summary
Paraphrasing (target language)
Note taking/outlining
Summarizing (Native language/target language)
Recursive listening (multiple tasks)
Inferential listening (drawing inferences, conclusions not presented overtly in the
    text)
Identifying sociolinguistic factors
Style shifting
Reaction/analysis activities
Creative elaboration activities
Source: Omaggio Hadley, 1993, p. 174.

Appendix B.

A Model for Teaching Interactive Listening and Reading

Stages	Lister/Reader Use of Text Meaning	Lister/Reader Use of Text Language	Class Activities
I. Pre-listening/ Pre-reading	Students preview the text, establish a purpose for listening to/reading the text, predict meaning.	Students use words and phrases as clues to meaning.	Students skim for the gist, scan for specific information, identify a purpose for listening to/reading the text, use their own background knowledge to explore the topic, and predict what they might learn in the text.
II. Identify main elements	Students identify main ideas, characters, settings, and events.	Students recognize discourse markers (adverbs, conjunctions, word order, clauses, phrases) that connect ideas and signal a shift in topic, setting, or event.	Students (in pairs or groups) discuss main ideas (perhaps following out-of-class preparation) by identifying the text topic and characters as well as the changes in events and settings of the story or text. Students match main ideas to specific sections of the text or select main ideas from a list of alternatives.

III. Identify details	Students listen and read intensively and connect main concepts to details.	Students identify examples of text details that support main concepts.	Using the main ideas identified in Stage II, students create a chart of main ideas and supporting details. Other activity: students select details from a list of alternatives.
IV. Organize/ revise main ideas/details	Students revise their summary of main ideas and supporting details.	Students use vocabulary from text to make changes in summary.	Students (in pairs or groups) compare charts developed in Stage III and verify that their organization of main ideas and details is consistent with the organization of the text and ideas presented in the text.
V. Recreate text	Students reconstruct textual information.	Students expand text phrases created earlier into sentences and paragraphs.	Following out-of-class preparation, students (in small groups) summarize or recreate the text.
VI. React to text/ explore intertextuality	Students give opinions and reactions to text and relate other texts to it.	Students use text as a reference to support their opinions.	Students discuss the text from their own points of view and share their opinions.

Source: Shrum & Glisan, 1994
(based on Swaffar, Arens, & Byrnes, 1991; Eskey, 1986; Phillips, 1984)

chapter **6**

Reading

Marva A. Barnett
University of Virginia

QUESTION 1: What is the current focus in reading research?

Discussion

Research on reading and on individual learner-as-reader differences focuses on a typical foreign language classroom scenario characterized by wide variations in students' comprehension ability and reading success, and almost limitless diversity in reading styles. Happily, the past decade has seen a substantial increase in the amount and seriousness of research on second-language reading, paralleled by a renewal of theoretical interest in the reading process. Many second-language reading theorists now see reading as an **interactive** mental process (Carrell et al., 1988; Grabe, 1988). To comprehend, readers not only see and think about the text before them, but also retrieve and examine relevant information from their memories. During this simultaneous process, readers consider the text, including letters, words, format, illustrations, context of its appearance, and so on (text-based elements, or "bottom-up" reading); they concurrently decide which aspects of everything they already know are pertinent to this text (reader-based elements or "top-down" reading). For instance, at the grammatical or syntactical level, readers might check the context to ascertain whether to read the word "plan" as a noun or a verb. At the level of word meanings, or semantics, they can determine whether the writer is being ironic or sarcastic. At the text level, they compare what they're reading with their appropriate background knowledge (what they already know about the text topic or structure). Moreover, it appears that this extremely complex process differs remarkably from one individual to another. The questions addressed here point to several underlying research questions: What comprehension strategies do second-language readers actually use when reading? Which seem to be most effective? Does teaching students strategies for reading help them read better? We can begin to answer these questions with results from several studies.

QUESTION 2: What comprehension strategies do second-language readers actually use when reading? Which seem most effective?

Discussion

Most of the research that directly studies reading strategies began in the 1980s and seems only now to be delineating what we mean by "strategies;" in fact, creating a complete reading-strategy inventory may prove to be difficult, if not impossible. The term "strategies" is generally taken to mean the conscious or unconscious mental operations involved when readers purposefully approach a text to make sense of what they read. Readers use strategies to engage actively in reading, and these strategies may be productive or unproductive. Such practical tactics can be either text-based ("local") strategies or extra-text ("global") strategies. Productive local strategies include, for example, recognizing cognates, skipping unknown words while using other contextual clues to establish meaning, and identifying the grammatical category of words to ascertain their function. Productive global strategies involve such things as using knowledge of the world to guide in inferring meaning, continuing to read for further clues when unsuccessful, and evaluating guesses as further meaning is comprehended.

Reading researchers now also categorize strategies as "cognitive" or "metacognitive." Readers who use cognitive strategies consciously apply their mental processes in order to understand what they're reading. The term "metacognitive strategy" or "awareness" refers to readers' ability to stand back from their own reading process, to recognize how well they're comprehending and how efficiently they're using various cognitive strategies (see the appendices for sample lists of strategies). Here are several examples of actual strategy use from two American students reading French (Barnett, 1989). The students were asked to read silently a French text about Clint Eastwood's election as mayor of a California town, saying aloud whatever they were thinking (thus generating what is called a "think-aloud protocol"). In the section quoted below, student JS frequently uses two cognitive reading strategies generally recognized as effective: (1) reading entire phrases before trying to figure them out and (2) considering the grammatical form (and syntactic uses) of unfamiliar words. We see two examples of each here (an ellipsis indicates a student's pause of about three seconds):

> [Sentence from original text: *Convaincre de vieilles dames vêtues de rose ou de vert pâle, de riches et paisibles retraitées qui ne se déplacent qu'en Bentley ou en Volvo, qu'il n'était pas un danger public.*
> Translation: To convince the elderly ladies dressed in pink or pale green, the rich and peaceful retirees who go about only in Bentleys or Volvos, that he wasn't a public danger.]

> JS: *Convaincre de vieilles dames vêtues de rose or de vert pâle.* I do not know what *convain— convaincre* means. Of old women *vêtues de rose ou de vert pâle, vêtues,* I'm not sure what that means, of rose or of pale green. So I would assume it would be something on their person, maybe an article of clothing or, no, of old, no, it doesn't have an article, so it wouldn't be .... It's probably an adjective or, 'cause it doesn't have an article, so it's not; I don't see an article, so I don't think it's a noun ... of the something of *riches* and *paisibles retraitées qui ne se déplacent qu'en Bentley ou en Volvo ....* I'm going back and rereading this sentence from the beginning to see if I ... can ....

In this think-aloud protocol, JS is also working on a metacognitive level: she constantly remarks about how much she thinks she is understanding. Given her high level of reading comprehension, it is surprising that her metacognitive awareness of her own strategy use is not entirely accurate. Just a few sentences later in this reading and think-aloud session, she says:

> I think what I should try to do is to read the whole sentence first, which I never do; I always try to translate word for word, and that usually doesn't work. Or not word for word, but from fragment to fragment, and sometimes when I read the whole sentence, it helps me make a little bit more sense of what I'm reading.

She apparently does not realize that she does indeed habitually consider entire sentences or clauses before analyzing them.

Another student's think-aloud protocol for the same reading passage shows an extremely different set of strategies:

> TW: *Convaincre,* I don't remember what that means either, of old women *vêtues,* again, I don't know that one either, of rose or pale green, riches and ... *retraitées,* it's kind of like retreat, *paisibles* sounds like plausible, who ... did not deplace themselves in a Bentley or a Volvo, and he ... ... was not in public danger. I'm not making much sense of this.

This segment shows a strong tendency to read word for word and to give up on figuring out unfamiliar words—cognitive strategies that generally prove relatively ineffective. The only metacognitive awareness that this student demonstrates here is a recognition of the fact that he is lost in the text.

This study indicates, as do several others, that readers who use a variety of productive strategies and who recognize and monitor their own strategy use (as does JS) tend to understand more of what they read in the foreign language than do students who use fewer cognitive and metacognitive strategies. It appears that successful readers keep the meaning of a passage in mind while reading, read (translate) in broad phrases, skip words they see as unimportant to total phrase meaning, and have a positive self-concept as readers. Unsuccessful readers lose the meaning of sentences as soon as they have decoded them, read (translate) in short phrases, tend to view all words as equally important, and have a negative self-concept as readers (Hosenfeld, 1977).

Readers' skill and strategy use in second-language reading seem to relate in complicated ways to their first-language reading. Proficient second-language readers monitor their comprehension much as do proficient first-language readers; less proficient second-language readers perform similarly to less proficient first-language readers (Block, 1992). They also more often use local reading strategies to understand a text, while more proficient second-language readers depend more on global comprehension strategies (see Appendix A for both types of strategies) (Carrell, 1989). Most readers use a unique combination of strategies, and no single set of processing strategies significantly or consistently contributes to success (Sarig, 1988). Strategic reading is more than a matter of knowing what strategy to use; it involves knowing how to use a strategy and how to orchestrate its use with other strategies (see the strategy list in Appendix B) (Anderson, 1991). We may quickly learn much more about individual strategy use with the help of computers. Software programs can help us better see the reading process (rather than the reading product that test results give us) by recording directly and unobtrusively how readers go about understanding: for instance, their use of a dictionary, their need for more contextual information, their curiosity about cultural allusions, their reading speed. Before we plunge too fast into what may be deep waters, however, we need to investigate how reading on a computer screen compares to reading a printed text—rather than simply assuming that they are the same.

In summary, our profession sees a sustained and growing interest in describing and analyzing the processes of second-language readers by using their conscious and unconscious comprehension strategies as windows onto these processes. Readers who use helpful combinations of strategies effectively do read better. The obvious, logical question for teachers, then, is whether we can teach students such productive strategy use.

QUESTION 3: Does teaching students specific reading strategies help them read better?

Discussion

Research steadily answers "yes" to this question. In fact, we can teach both cognitive and metacognitive strategies successfully and have our students generally read more efficiently as a result of that training. Hosenfeld and high school teacher colleagues (1981), after finding tentative positive results in strategy training, offer a sequence of activities to teach reading strategies. The authors advocate first teaching students to think aloud, or self-report, as they read in order to discover which strategies they are using; teachers use the Interviewer Guide for Reading Strategies (see Appendix C) to categorize the strategy use. After determining where their students need help, teachers design a series of classroom or homework activities to teach students the strategies they need. The activity sequence modeled in this article teaches how to infer word meanings from context by first helping students identify useful strategies and then providing exercises.

Following upon Hosenfeld's work, more recent studies have consistently found strategy training to be at least partially effective in both foreign-language and ESL settings. Students with a low reading ability benefit from instruction in reading strategies more than middle- or high-ability readers, and combinations of strategies are more effective than strategies used in isolation (Kern, 1988). Strategy training is probably most effective when the instructor believes in it (Barnett, 1988); but it clearly improves readers' morale and confidence.

The focus on cognitive strategy development illustrated by these studies is paralleled by an equally concentrated attention to students' metacognitive awareness of how they read. Reading comprehension seems to depend not only on familiarity with text content, but also on readers' ability to monitor what they understand in order to take appropriate strategic action. Teachers can introduce students to the concept and language of routine comprehension monitoring and teach specific monitoring and comprehension strategies (Casanave, 1988). The effectiveness of any training method may depend not only upon the way the teacher measures reading comprehension, but also on differences in students' learning styles (Carrell et al., 1989).

Future experiments may well study the details of who benefits most and why, the precise relative importance of each type of strategy, the significance of local versus global strategies to different types of readers, and so on. In the meantime, teachers can use some of the existing research methods as valuable tools to analyze their students' strategies and to give them an insight into their own reading process. Students can think aloud, or self-report, while reading to demonstrate how and what they understand (Casanave, 1988; Hosenfeld et al., 1981). More and more, software programs will be able to record similar information (Hulstijn, 1993). Traditional reading tests can be interspersed with activities in which students write what they understand and recall from a text ("recall protocols"), while teachers analyze these recalls to decide what students should be taught next (Bernhardt, 1991). We can raise students' metacognitive awareness by asking them directly what reading strategies they think they use (Barnett, 1989).

The past fifteen years have seen new second-language reading research spin off from serious inquiry about first-language reading. The ongoing interest in reading strategies and in the relationship between first- and second-language reading ability and strategy use is only part of that field, and much research remains to be done. We can, however, say with some certainty that individual students do indeed read in very different ways, that some reading strategies are more effective than others, that we can profitably teach students to use certain cognitive and metacognitive strategies, that poor readers can become better readers. We need to keep in mind that different types of texts can require different types of reading, that reading strategies are only part of what goes into reading comprehension, and that knowing a variety of strategies and being able to combine them efficiently and appropriately is central to reading effectively. In sum, good readers use good critical thinking skills—something we all probably aim to teach all the time.

Bibliography

Anderson, N. J. 1991. "Individual Differences in Strategy Use in Second Language Reading and Testing." *Modern Language Journal* 75: 460-72.

Barnett, M. A. 1988. "Teaching Reading Strategies: How Methodology Affects Language Course Articulation." *Foreign Language Annals* 21: 109-19.

Barnett, M. A. 1989. *More Than Meets the Eye: Foreign Language Reading, Theory and Practice.* Englewood Cliffs, NJ: Prentice Hall.

Bernhardt, E. B. 1991. *Reading Development in a Second Language: Theoretical, Empirical, and Classroom Perspectives.* Norwood, NJ: Ablex.

Block, E. L. 1992. "See How They Read: Comprehension Monitoring of L1 and L2 Readers." *TESOL Quarterly* 26: 319-43.

Carrell, P. L. 1989. "Metacognitive Awareness and Second Language Reading." *Modern Language Journal* 73: 121-34.

Carrell, P., J. Devine, and D. Eskey, eds. 1988. *Interactive Approaches to Second Language Reading.* New York: Cambridge University Press.

Carrell, P. L., B. G. Pharis, and J. C. Liberto. 1989. "Metacognitive Strategy Training for ESL Reading." *TESOL Quarterly* 23: 647-78.

Casanave, C. P. 1988. "Comprehension Monitoring in ESL Reading: A Neglected Essential." *TESOL Quarterly* 22: 283-302.

Davis, J. N., L. Carbon Gorell, R. R. Kline, and G. Hsieh. 1992. "Readers and Foreign Languages: A Survey of Undergraduate Attitudes toward the Study of Literature." *Modern Language Journal* 76: 320-32.

Grabe, W. 1988. "Reassessing the Term 'Interactive,'" in P. Carrell et al., eds., *Interactive Approaches to Second Language Reading.* New York: Cambridge University Press.

Grellet, F. 1981. *Developing Reading Skills: A Practical Guide to Reading Comprehension Exercises.* Cambridge: Cambridge University Press. (Also, ERIC Document Reproduction Service No. ED 207 347.)

Hosenfeld, C. 1977. "A Preliminary Investigation of the Reading Strategies of Successful and Nonsuccessful Second Language Learners." *System* 5: 110-23.

Hosenfeld, C., V. Arnold, J. Kirchofer, J. Laciura, and L. Wilson. 1981. "Second Language Reading: A Curricular Sequence for Teaching Reading Strategies." *Foreign Language Annals* 14: 415-22.

Hulstijn, J. H. 1993. "When Do Foreign-Language Readers Look up the Meaning of Unfamiliar Words? The Influence of Task and Learner Variables." *Modern Language Journal* 77: 139-47.

Kern, R. G. 1989. "Second Language Reading Strategy Instruction: Its Effects on Comprehension and Word Inference Ability." *Modern Language Journal* 73: 135-49.

Phillips, J. K. 1984. "Practical Implications of Recent Research in Reading." *Foreign Language Annals* 8: 227-32.

Sarig, G. 1988. "High-level Reading in the First and in the Foreign Language: Some Comparative Process Data," in J. Devine, P. L. Carrell, and D. E. Eskey, eds., *Research in Reading in English as a Second Language.* Washington, DC: TESOL.

Swaffar, J., K. M. Arens, and H. Byrnes. 1991. *Reading for Meaning: An Integrated Approach to Language Learning.* Englewood Cliffs, NJ: Prentice-Hall.

Young, D. J. 1989. "A Systematic Approach to Foreign Language Reading Instruction: What Does the Research Suggest?" *Hispania* 72: 755-62.

Appendix A

Sample Metacognitive Questionnaire
[Slightly adapted from P. L. Carrell, 1989]

The following statements are about silent reading in Spanish. Please indicate the level of your agreement or disagreement with each statement by circling the appropriate number: 1 indicates strong agreement, 5 indicates strong disagreement. [The numbers have been omitted here to save space].

When reading silently in Spanish,

1.   I am able to anticipate what will come next in the text.

2.   I am able to recognize the difference between main points and supporting details.

3.   I am able to relate information which comes next in the text to previous information in the text.

4.   I am able to question the significance or truthfulness of what the author says.

5.   I am able to use my prior knowledge and experience to understand the content of the text I am reading.

6.   I have a good sense of when I understand something and when I do not.

When reading silently in Spanish, if I don't understand something,

7.   I keep on reading and hope for clarification further on.

8.   I reread the problematic part.

9.   I go back to a point before the problematic part and reread from there.

10.   I look up unknown words in a dictionary.

11.   I give up and stop reading.

When I read silently in Spanish, the things I do to read effectively are to focus on

12.   mentally sounding out parts of the words.

13.   understanding the meaning of each word.

14.   getting the overall meaning of the text.

15.   being able to pronounce each whole word.

16.   the grammatical structures.

17.   relating the text to what I already know about the topic.

18.   looking up words in the dictionary.

19.   the details of the content.

20.   the organization of the text.

When I read silently in Spanish, things that make the reading difficult are

21.   the sounds of the individual words.

22.   pronunciation of the words.

23.   recognizing the words.

24.   the grammatical structures.

25.   the alphabet.

26.   relating the text to what I already know about the topic.

27.   getting the overall meaning of the text.

28.   the organization of the text.

The best reader I know in Spanish is a good reader because of his/her ability to

29.   recognize words.

30.   sound out words.

31.   understand the overall meaning of a text.

32.   use a dictionary.

33.   guess at word meanings.

34.   integrate the information in the text with what he/she already knows.

35.   focus on the details of the content.

36.   grasp the organization of the text.

Appendix B

Categories of Processing Strategies
(used in a reading test situation)
[Slightly adapted from N.J. Anderson, 1991]

I. Supervising [mostly metacognitive] strategies. The reader:
1. refers to the experimental task.
2. recognizes loss of concentration.
3. states failure to understand a portion of the text.
4. states success in understanding a portion of the text.
5. adjusts reading rate in order to increase comprehension.
6. formulates a question.
7. makes a prediction about the meaning of a words of about text content.
8. refers to lexical items that impede comprehension.
9. confirms/disconfirms an inference.
10. refers to the previous passage.
11. responds affectively to text content.

II. Support strategies. The reader:
12. skips unknown words.
13. expresses a need for a dictionary.
14. skims reading material for a general understand.
15. scans reading material for a specific word or phrase.
16. visualizes.

III. Paraphrase strategies. The reader:
17. uses cognates between first and second language to comprehend.
18. breaks lexical items into parts.
19. paraphrases.
20. translates a words or a phrase into the native language.
21. extrapolates from information presented in the text.
22. speculates beyond the information presented in the text.

IV. Strategies for establishing coherence in text. The reader:
23. rereads.
24. uses context clues to interpret a word or phrase.
25. reacts to author's style or text's surface structure.
26. reads ahead.
27. uses background knowledge.
28. acknowledges lack of background knowledge.
29. relates the stimulus sentence to personal experience.

Appendix C

Interviewer Guide for Reading Strategies
[Slightly adapted from C. Hosenfeld et al., 1981]

General Reading Behavior
* Rarely translates; Guesses contextually
* Translates; Guesses contextually
* Translates; Guesses noncontextually
* Translates; Rarely guesses

Observed Strategies   **Comments**

1. Keeps meaning in mind.
2. Skips unknown words (guesses contextually).
3. Uses context in preceding and succeeding sentences and paragraphs.
4. Identifies grammatical category of words.
5. Evaluates guesses.
6. Reads title (makes inferences).
7. Continues if unsuccessful.
8. Recognizes cognates.
9. Uses knowledge of the world.
10. Analyzes unknown words.
11. Reads as though he or she expects the text to make sense.
12. Reads to identify meaning rather than words.
13. Takes chances in order to identify meaning.
14. Uses illustration.
15. Uses side-gloss.
16. Uses glossary as last resort.
17. Looks up words correctly.
18. Skips unnecessary words.
19. Follows through with proposed solutions.
20. Uses a variety of types of context clues.

chapter 7

Speaking

Myriam Met
Montgomery County Public Schools

QUESTION 1: What is involved in becoming a proficient speaker?

Discussion

Speaking is one of the most difficult and complex skills for language learners. In most situations, speaking involves more than talk—most speaking tasks are interactive, involving more than one speaker in a constant interplay of comprehension and production. Speaking requires interpreting the meanings conveyed by others, expressing one's own meanings, and negotiating meanings, so that each speaker understands and is understood.

In the 1960s and 1970s, it was fashionable to speak of "learning objectives" which students would "master." Today, foreign language professionals recognize that oral proficiency—the ability to communicate in the language—is an evolutionary process in which students gain increasing control of the target language through a variety of experiences: direct instruction, internalization through input, individual reflection, and interaction with others. The ultimate goal for language learners is to develop a level of control which results in native-like proficiency.

The components of communication which students need to control are numerous. Traditionally, learning a language was viewed as control of grammar knowledge: if students knew the grammar rules, they knew the language, and should thus be able to speak it. Today, we know that oral language use is far more complex than simply knowledge of grammar rules. In order to speak, the student has to synthesize and gain control over a significant amount of knowledge and a number of skills, which both include and extend beyond grammar. Proficient speakers, for example, have lexical knowledge that allows for both flexibility and precision. They are able to choose appropriately from a variety of ways to encode their message; they tailor their language to different contexts and different listeners and can accurately convey what they want to say. The speech of proficient language users also reflects the cultural meanings and associations that underlie even common, everyday words such as "home," "work," or "family," as well as the cultural and social protocols that govern communication contexts (how to be polite, how to take conversational turns, how to adjust language to the situation and the social relationships of speakers). Proficient speakers are able to put their words together effectively and advantageously in ways that communicate not only the broad general and global message, but the specific and subtle as well. They are sensitive to meanings conveyed by such things as intonation, rhythm, and modulation and can convey and interpret meaning through non-verbal modes, such as body language, gestures, facial expressions, and distance. They maintain a natural flow and pace in expression of meaning and are able to manage repairs when communication breaks down. The knowledge and skills that contribute to proficiency in speaking must be synthesized instantaneously, a significant challenge for language learners.

Language learners, as developing speakers, will show different degrees of control of these characteristics at various stages of their learning. The many elements of language over which students need to develop control in order to be proficient speakers have been classified into four major categories of communicative competence:

1) **grammatical competence** (knowledge of vocabulary, pronunciation, morphology, and syntax),

2) **sociolinguistic competence** (the ability to adjust one's communication to the situation, task, or role of participants),

3) **discourse competence** (the ability to combine utterances so that there is cohesion and coherence within and between sentences), and

4) **strategic competence** (the ability to enhance the effectiveness of one's communication or to perform communicative tasks which may surpass one's linguistic repertoire by paraphrasing, circumlocuting, using repair strategies, etc.) (Canale and Swain, 1980; Canale, 1983).

Considering these factors, it is no wonder that developing proficient users of a foreign language is a challenging task for teachers. Of course, there is no one best way to teach speaking. We do know, however, that a number of factors contribute to the development of speaking ability. Among the most significant are: varied, extensive, and intensive opportunities to focus on meaning as one hears the language spoken naturally in authentic contexts; an emphasis on meaningful, purposeful language use in classroom tasks; and frequent and varied opportunities to interact in the language. We will examine each of these factors in greater detail below.

QUESTION 2:   What is the role of internalization in producing proficient speakers?

Discussion

Language is initially acquired through exposure to input that is meaningful and comprehensible (Krashen, 1982). In order for students to produce language sponta- neously, they must first understand it. Internalizing the relationship between meaning and the forms used to convey it and storing this relationship in long-term memory are essential for production: Students simply can't spontaneously produce language they don't first understand and remember. Through extensive and varied exposure to the language, exposure which makes the ways of transmitting meanings in the second language accessible and understandable, and through interaction with others, students come to develop an internalized representation of how the language conveys meanings. Cognitive psychologists call this process *constructing knowledge* (Resnick, 1989). The process of constructing knowledge of the many sub-systems of the language is complex. [See Glisan, this volume.] It is clear, however, that this process is a prerequisite for the development of speaking proficiency.

The need for students to internalize meanings before they can realistically be expected to produce them orally has a number of implications for classroom practice:

1) The target language needs to be used as much as possible in the classroom. Obviously, if learning to speak is dependent upon the extent of one's exposure to the new language, the more classroom time is spent in English, the less exposure to the foreign language students will have.

2) Extensive teacher use of the target language is beneficial only if it is comprehensible. Decontextualized lectures ("talking head" activities in which speakers talk without any visuals, body language, or other cues to meaning) and other forms of target language talk that do not allow students to access meaning are unlikely to result in increased understand- ing of the target language.

3) Use of the target language, particularly at the early stages of language development, should be supported with techniques that allow students to assign meaning to what they hear: pictures, other visual aids, body language, and videos are all ways of providing students with clues to meaning.

4) Comprehension precedes production. Activities in which new vocabulary or, in particular, structures, are presented in a variety of contexts not only enable students to assign meaning to what they hear but are more likely to result in the development of oral proficiency when they precede activities that demand productive use of language.

5) Students should be asked to demonstrate their ability to discriminate meanings before producing them. For example, the student of English who does not understand the difference between "walk" and "walked" will be unlikely to produce the correct past tense ending when it is needed.

6) Students can be assisted to move from input through intake to constructing meaning through a carefully planned and implemented sequence of instructional activities (Adair-Hauck, Donato, and Cumo, 1994).

QUESTION 3: What role does practice play in learning to speak a language?

Discussion

To become proficient speakers of another language, students need to engage in classroom activities that allow for meaningful, purposeful language use. As discussed earlier, research suggests that comprehensible input is a necessary condition for the development of speaking skills. However, by itself it is not sufficient. Students also need to engage in comprehensible output, that is, in practice that allows them to express their own meanings (Swain, 1985). Comprehensible output provides learners the opportunity to test the validity of their hypotheses about how the language works. By striving to make their output comprehensible through interaction with others, learners develop strategic competence. Output is also critical for guiding students to see the relationship between form, accuracy, and meaning.

As many students (and their teachers) have discovered, **knowing** the language may be a deceptively simple goal in comparison to **using** what one knows. Because speaking requires the spontaneous integration and application of knowledge in numerous domains, knowing the rules and vocabulary does not necessarily result in fluent, coherent, and accurate utterances, particularly when students are at the novice or intermediate stages of proficiency. The complexity of synthesizing so much knowledge places significant demands on learners. As a result, it is unreasonable to expect students to synthesize all their knowledge with a high degree of accuracy. Rather, our goal should be successively accurate approximations of native-like language use over time.

The complexities and demands of knowledge synthesis into performance means that classroom activities should emphasize opportunities to *use* knowledge and skills. This emphasis on integration of knowledge and skills into performance is not unlike learning to play the violin or to swim. While there are important skills and knowledge to be acquired (e.g., musical notation, scales, appropriate arm and leg strokes for swimming), these are only useful when they are put together to accomplish a meaningful task such as performing a piece of music or crossing the width of the pool. In other words, knowing how to read music or when to breathe when swimming has little value except when synthesized to accomplish the stated goal. Similarly, knowing vocabulary or the rules of grammar is of little use if one cannot use them to interact in the language. Some aspects of learners' knowledge will contribute more to the quality of their musical or swimming performance than will others at given points of their skill development (e.g., their use of the bow may be better than their fingering technique; their arm stroke may be more effective than leg strokes). Similarly, a wide range of vocabulary may contribute more to the communicative abilities of novice learners than may their knowledge of tenses. Lastly, and perhaps most importantly, the purpose of continued instruction and practice is to improve one's overall performance by successive improvement in each of the knowledge and skill areas that contributes to performance. Clearly then, classroom speaking activities must allow students to synthesize their knowledge and skills through meaningful use.

Proficiency in speaking a foreign language requires frequent and varied opportunities for interaction (Shrum and Glisan, 1994). Communicating is more than just talk— it requires interpreting, expressing, and negotiating meaning (Savignon, 1991). In most cases, communicating means two or more people interacting. This interaction is in sharp contrast to the kinds of speaking activities which were common in teaching methods of the past. Speaking proficiency does not develop from repeating after the teacher, or from engaging in rote drills in which students merely parrot or recite as required, or from reciting memorized dialogues aloud. While there may be legitimate debate about the merits of these activities for some purposes, it would be difficult to suggest that such activities provide practice in communicating interactively with one or more conversation partners (Larsen-Freeman, 1986).

Interaction is important because, in real life, speaking is part of a complex process in which partners respond to others, strive to understand, and check to make sure they are being understood. The subtle (and usually imperceptible) back-and-forth process of checking to see if one is understanding and being understood is called the negotiation of meaning. All of us do it all the time, whether in our native language or in another language. For language learners, negotiation of meaning is an important part of the internalization process.

Frequent and sustained opportunities for interaction provide students with practice in both producing meaning and in checking the comprehensibility of their messages (Lang, 1993). When students interact with one or more conversation partners, they "test the waters"—that is, they test the accuracy of the hypotheses they have constructed about how the foreign language conveys meanings. If their utterances are accepted and responded to appropriately by others, students can be relatively certain that their message has been conveyed and interpreted. On the other hand, the lack of response, a quizzical look, or an outright request for clarification (e.g., "Could you repeat that?" "Could you explain?" or simply "WHAT?") may be a clear indicator that the message needs repair. The feedback provided by interaction with others is critical to the continued growth of students' abilities to communicate effectively (Doughty and Pica, 1986; Swain, 1985; Lang, 1983).

Interaction is also important because most real-life speaking tasks involve interacting with others. Our students will have limited opportunities to engage in one-way speaking tasks (e.g., leaving messages on answering machines, giving lectures, speaking on television). Most of the speaking they will do will involve others—conversation partners with whom they will interact on a personal level, engage in thoughtful discussion and debate, or with whom they will negotiate some type of transaction. Transactions such as buying toothpaste, obtaining a ticket to a show, or agreeing on the way to solve a mutual problem are real-life tasks which will require two-way communication and which will be enacted with speakers of various ages, backgrounds, and tolerances for non-native language use. Students will need to have numerous opportunities to engage in interactions and transactions with various partners under conditions which progress from extremely sheltered and classroom-like, to increasingly varied and unpredictable (Omaggio Hadley, 1993).

QUESTION 4:   How can classroom practice be designed to yield maximum benefit?

Discussion

Communication generally involves the exchange of new information. In real-life communication, there is usually an information or opinion gap—the knowledge or opinions of one conversation partner are unknown to the other. Communication fills these gaps: we learn about people's opinions and preferences, or we find out new information (Larsen-Freeman, 1986). Unlike classrooms, where teachers frequently know the answers to the questions they ask, in real life, people rarely say things that their listener already knows (Long and Porter, 1985). For example, we would rarely ask someone to whom we were talking, "Are you a boy or a girl?" In real life, we also avoid telling others something they already know. For example, when we begin to tell a story, and we see our listener nodding actively as we speak, we might ask, "Oh, did I tell you this already?" If the answer is yes, we change topics or shift the conversation.

Filling an information or opinion gap is a major purpose for communicating. Furthermore, the information or opinions that conversation partners share always have real meaning. These two characteristics of communication—meaning and purpose—are essential characteristics of speaking activities in the classroom. Students will benefit most from tasks in which real meanings are conveyed, and in which students perceive a purpose for speaking.

The language-practice activities that are found in many commercially produced textbooks range from meaningless/purposeless to highly meaningful and purposeful. These activities can be placed on a continuum. (The following discussion is adapted from Littlewood, 1981.) At one end are rote drills, those that can be performed without even knowing the meanings of the words. A rote vocabulary drill may substitute different items in the blank as follows: I have a book. (pencil, ruler, whatchamacallit). Even without knowing the meanings of "pencil," "ruler," or "whatchamacallit," students can accurately substitute the noun in the correct place and accurately produce a new sentence. Not only is there no meaning involved, there is no purpose other than to do what the teacher says. Students have no control over their output; the teacher has complete control. In a contextualized rote drill, the sentences may be linked to one another in some way, but there is still an absence of meaning or purpose, and there is still no student control over output. For example, students may be asked to put the following sentences in the past tense: I wake up. I get dressed. I go to school. I gromble. Regardless of the meaning of the sentence, there is only one correct way of completing the task—even for a meaningless verb like gromble, students know they must say, "grombled."

Further along the continuum, tasks may require meaning for their completion, but teachers still control student output. For example, students may be given a list of daily activities and be asked to describe how they spent their day by ordering the list and putting the tasks in the past tense: I . . . (get dressed, arrive at school, wake up, ride the school bus). In all three task types described thus far, teacher control of student out-put means that there is only one possible correct answer.

At the other end of the continuum are those tasks that involve meaning and purpose and ultimately leave the students themselves in control of their output. For most classroom tasks, the purpose should parallel a real-life purpose for which the student might actually need to use the language (Omaggio Hadley, 1993; Larsen-Freeman, 1986). In this sense, purpose has an element of authenticity to it—authentic to the real-life purposes for which we use language. Asking students to pretend to be travel agents and convince clients to choose a destination in a target culture country may be open-ended and meaningful, but it is certainly not "authentic" to the middle- and high-school student who does not even know how to role-play a travel agent in English! Tasks at this end of the continuum, then, are truly communicative when they have meaning, purpose, and involve a real exchange of information or opinions. Student answers are unpredictable, and no two students are expected to answer in the same way. One way to recognize textbook activities of this type is by reference to the answer key found in the textbook's Teacher's Edition. For these activities, the answer key will indicate, "Answers will vary." Some examples of this type of task are: Tell your partner three things you did yesterday before 10 a.m. and the order in which you did them. Find out your partner's food preferences and compare them to your own.

Research does not suggest whether all of the various task types on the continuum are necessary for the development of speaking proficiency, nor the extent to which each should be included in classroom practice. It is clear, however, that if students are to become effective at real-life communication outside the classroom, they will need extensive practice inside the classroom that prepares them for the real world. Students will need to engage in classroom practice that allows for control of their output—activities that involve a real exchange of information/opinions, require the expression of real meanings, and serve a real communicative purpose (Omaggio Hadley, 1993; Shrum and Glisan, 1994). In real life, "answers will vary." Earlier, we saw that speaking is challenging because it requires students to synthesize knowledge and skills extemporaneously in a variety of language domains. If students spend their classroom practice time producing predictable, predetermined answers to questions that have little personal meaning for them, the kind of synthesis required in real-life communication will be difficult for them to achieve. Information-gap activities are one type of communicative task that is very useful for providing meaningful and purposeful language practice. Such activities are most effective when each person involved (whether pair, group, or even whole class) has information needed by the other(s). Tasks in which the information known by one or more participants is not needed to complete the task result in fewer modified interactions—modifications through which students seek or provide clarification, comprehension checks, etc. (Doughty and Pica, 1986). As we saw earlier, students need to negotiate meaning and develop strategic competence in order to learn their new language, and properly constructed information-gap tasks can contribute substantially to that goal.

Open-ended, communicative tasks can be found in a variety of sources. Although teachers should be quite cautious about textbook claims that label tasks as communicative (even when they are not), many textbooks today do provide the kinds of practice students will need. Teachers should analyze exercises to carefully determine which ones masquerade as communication (when they are really predictable-response exercises) and which activities truly engage students as active creators and conveyors of meaning. Situation cards, either teacher-made or commercial products, are frequently a good source of communicative language practice. Good situation cards provide a context for a speaking task in which the purpose, meaning, and conversation partner are clearly specified. The most useful of these tasks are those that simulate a situation in which students might actually find themselves (for example, "You've lost your little brother at the zoo. Describe what he looks like and what he is wearing to a police officer.").

Communicative tasks should be structured and have a clearly defined outcome. They should require a real exchange of meaning, and to the fullest extent possible, involve truth value for the student. Beyond the novice level, students need practice in different types of communicative tasks, such as narratives, face-to-face transactions, descriptions, giving instructions, etc. These different types of tasks require different ways of organizing and communicating information (Richards, 1985). Advancing learners also need interactive practice that enhances the appropriateness of their language use: They need practice in opening and closing interactions and transactions; they need to know how speakers of the target language signal conversational turn-taking; how to take or keep the floor; how to interrupt; and how to use paraphrasing and circumlocution when their intended message exceeds the capacity of their linguistic repertoire.

In creating communicative classroom tasks, teachers may be guided by questions such as, "When in real-life would my students need the vocabulary/grammar/cultural knowledge I want them to practice? What are the real-life situations in which my students may find themselves and what kinds of classroom practice can I provide that will enable them to communicate effectively?" Asking questions in this way is very different from more traditional approaches to task development. In grammar-driven methodologies, exercises were designed to practice grammar and to develop accuracy.

In a proficiency orientation, activities serve to provide practice in communicating, and grammar is at the service of communication.

The importance of output in language development has a number of implications for the classroom:

1) Students need extensive practice in using what they know.

2) Instructional time should be allocated so that there is maximum opportunity for students to integrate and apply knowledge they have acquired.

3) The majority of classroom practice activities should involve a true exchange of meaning.

4) The majority of classroom practice activities should have a valid purpose for communicating.

5) Classroom practice activities should allow students increasing control over what they say. Such activities will probably not have one right answer, and student answers will vary.

QUESTION 5: What is the role of pair and group work in the foreign language classroom?

Discussion

The importance of providing opportunities for classroom interaction has led to the popularity of pair and group work in foreign language classrooms. Pair and group work is an effective way of providing sustained and frequent opportunities for students to practice speaking to others (Long and Porter, 1985). Such student-to-student communication, as we have seen, can contribute significantly to improved speaking proficiency. In recent years, educators across all disciplines have come to emphasize pair and group work as an effective way of structuring classroom tasks.

Let's take a moment to compare the classroom where students talk only to the teacher (the teacher-centered classroom) with one where there is frequent student to-student interaction through pair or group structures. In all classrooms, when there is only teacher-centered instruction, it is easy for some students to dominate while others withdraw from participation. Unfortunately, in foreign language classrooms, this domination results in the fact that the people who need the least practice (the teacher and those students who know the most) get the most practice, while those who could use the most practice don't get it. The teacher gets at least half the turns—by asking questions of students or commenting on their answers (Long and Porter, 1985). In addition, the students who are competent speakers or more motivated learners tend to volunteer and get called on more frequently than those who can't or don't want to speak (Doughty and Pica, 1986). In the teacher-centered environment, it is also difficult to know how much all students know, not just what is known by just those who recite. In contrast, pair and group tasks ensure that students are more participatory (Nerenz and Knop, 1982). And, by circulating throughout the room, teachers can more accurately assess the speaking proficiency of a larger number of students.

In the foreign language classroom, teacher-centered instruction limits the amount of "air-time" available for students to practice their speaking skills since, as we have seen, the teacher gets much of the air time. Further, it provides limited input since students hear only teacher talk. Teacher-centered instruction also limits opportunities for practicing the social language skills and contexts characteristic of peer-to-peer communication.

There is little doubt that pair and group work can further the speaking goals of the foreign language curriculum. Unfortunately, managing pair and group work so that students stay in the language and remain on task requires teacher knowledge and skill. Too often, attempts to institute pair and group speaking tasks result in students' using English most of the time or, even worse, using English to talk about topics unrelated to instructional purposes (Nerenz and Knop, 1982). The management of pair and group work and the relationship between good management and cooperative learning are discussed below.

First, it may be helpful to distinguish between cooperative learning and pair/group work. While all cooperative learning involves students working in pairs or small groups, there are factors beyond the mere use of pair/group tasks that have been shown to influence the effectiveness of such tasks (Johnson, Johnson, Johnson, and Ray, 1986). By definition, cooperative learning requires collaboration to achieve a goal. In the foreign language classroom, an appropriate group goal might be that all students be able to exchange personal and biographical information about themselves and others (e.g., identifying one's name and describing physical characteristics) or to narrate a simple past event. Students may engage in teacher-designed communicative tasks in their groups, practicing their speaking (and listening) skills, and providing feedback to one another, so that all can ultimately perform appropriately on the stated goal. In the cooperative learning research, collaboration and reliance on other group members to achieve a group goal is called "positive interdependence" (Kagan, 1992; Johnson et al., 1986).

Another characteristic of cooperative learning is individual accountability (Salvin, 1983). Students must know they are each ultimately accountable for their own learning.

Each student will be held accountable through the evaluation procedures established by the teacher. Therefore, each student needs to strive to learn and do as much as possible—there can be no "hitchhikers" resting on the work of one or two "chauffeurs." Other characteristics of cooperative learning include the explicit development of group processing and social skills (Johnson, et al., 1986).

The above discussion should not be interpreted to suggest that unless all the characteristics of cooperative settings are in place, teachers should not plan for student pair or group work. Rather, the extent to which the various elements are included and addressed may contribute to improving the extent to which pair/group work enhances students' language proficiency.

Effective management of pair/group work is, in part, related to the characteristics of cooperative learning environments. Good management will thus ensure that students stay on task and speak in the foreign language. First, teachers need to build into each activity individual accountability and positive interdependence. Students need to know how they will be accountable for the work they do during group time, and have a reason for cooperating with others. Individual accountability can be achieved in a variety of ways. Students may be given worksheets to complete as part of the group task. For example, let's suppose students are to interview the members of the group (e.g., "Find out the birthday of each member of your group." or "Find out how old each person in your group was when he/she began to walk."). Students may complete an interview sheet which includes the interview question, the names of the persons interviewed, and their answers. Teachers may collect the interview sheets and simply check to see that they were completed. Or, the teacher may grade the completed worksheets (either those of randomly selected students or of the entire class). Alternatively (or in addition), the teacher may use the answers provided as the basis for a follow up task the next day. Students may be told that the product of their group work will be the basis for another in-class or homework task. For example, the answers given by one's partner in an interview task may be the basis for a composition to be written about that person. If students stray off task or ask/answer questions in English, the follow-up task will be exceedingly difficult for them to do. Of course, an age-old way of holding individuals accountable for learning/working during group time is the quiz or test. Teachers may alert students to the possibility that the speaking task carried out during pair work parallels the speaking task on the test. The more engaged and on-task students remain during pair time—that is, the more earnestly they exploit the chance to practice with their partner—the better they will probably perform on the speaking test.

Positive interdependence can be built into pair/group tasks by giving each group member a specific role to perform, or assigning individual students to carry out part of the task. Some teachers distribute materials or information among individual team members so the task cannot be completed without everyone's contribution. Another way to insure positive interdependence is to let students know that at the conclusion of group time, one member from the pair or group will be called on to answer for the team. Therefore, everyone must be sure that everyone else can give an appropriate answer in the foreign language.

One management technique which is very helpful in keeping novice (and even intermediate) students on task and in the target language is to place short time limits on pair or group tasks. A short time limit encourages students to get to work quickly and to use their group time efficiently. Moreover, short time limits tend to keep students in the language because students know they won't have time to do the task twice—once in English and then translated into the foreign language. Lastly, novice students, in particular, don't know enough of the language to fill a long time period—they can hardly fill even five minutes with nothing but target language talk. For them, a long time allocation for a pair or group task is an invitation to use English. A number of cooperative learning structures and formats developed by researchers such as Kagan (1992) and Slavin (1983) are particularly adaptable to foreign language classrooms. These can be used to structure speaking tasks that promote participation by all group members, allow for meaningful, purposeful, communication that simulates real-life language use, yet at the same time ensure that there is positive interdependence and individual accountability. (See Shrum and Glisan, 1994, for examples.) In addition, many of these structures can be chained together to link low-level speaking tasks (e.g., brainstorming vocabulary needed, practicing the grammar points in a limited communicative context) with more complex, multi-skill, multi-step interactive or transactional tasks. Preparatory activities such as brainstorming facilitate performance on more complex speaking tasks. They "prime the pump," insuring that students are explicitly reminded of the language knowledge and skills in their repertoire that they will need to call on in performing a speaking task (Nerenz and Knop, 1982). Since we know that speaking requires the extemporaneous integration of knowledge from a number of domains, bringing that knowledge to the fore provides the "think time" which some students will need to enhance their performance.

QUESTION 6: How and when should student errors be corrected?

Discussion

Many teachers have voiced concern about how to correct student errors in teacher-centered tasks. Others are also concerned that student errors may go largely uncorrected during pair/group work. Unfortunately, research provides few hard and fast answers to these concerns.

Most researchers today have turned away from the question "Should errors be corrected?" to more useful questions such as: "What does it tell us when a student makes an error?" "Should some errors be corrected and others not?" "What kinds of error correction are most effective?" "When should errors be corrected and by whom?"

For many, student "errors" are not mistakes stemming from incomplete mastery but rather a reflection of the student's progress in constructing an understanding of how to create meaning in this new language. As students have increasing exposure to the language and become more proficient language users, they are better able to internalize meanings in the target language. As we saw earlier, the process of internalization is continually involved in language development. Through this process, students re-construct their understanding of the language, improve their language performance and thereby, eliminate the "errors."

Other researchers suggest that some errors are more important to correct than others. They have pointed out that certain errors rarely interfere with effective communication and that native speakers react differently to different types of errors. Given the impossibility of correcting and perfecting everything all at once, these researchers suggest that error correction focus on those errors which negatively affect native speakers or which otherwise represent significant obstacles to getting the message across. [For discussion, see Hendrickson, 1978.]

Lastly, researchers have questioned whether some types of error correction are more likely than others to improve student performance. Error correction is more broadly defined than the pinpointing of explicit mistakes or the direct provision to students of the "right response." Numerous types of error correction have been identified, ranging from simply repeating the student's utterance in correct form, to negative feedback which requires the student to negotiate the meaning of his/her message (e.g., "Sorry, I didn't understand."), to "enhanced input" in which the teacher makes repeated overt use of the correct forms in his/her input to students. [For further discussion of the research on error correction, see Mings, 1993.]

Although research provides little solid evidence related to error correction, most practitioners today are guided by a widely held belief that errors made by students in activities focused on acquiring grammar rules should be correctly explicitly. In contrast, when students are engaged in communicative tasks where the focus is on interacting in the foreign language, teachers should not interrupt students to correct them. Many teachers find it useful to make note of those errors made frequently by students and use their observations to design language lessons and tasks which provide further instruction and practice.

Some teachers have voiced concern that students who are engaged in pair or group work make errors which go uncorrected. Others worry that students will learn each other's mistakes. Neither of these concerns is supported by research (Long and Porter, 1985). First, as we have just seen, many researchers suggest that errors not be corrected during interactive, communicative tasks, and pair/group tasks are almost always interactive and communicative. Studies have also shown that students are able to correct one another, and do not learn each other's mistakes (Nunan, 1991). Further, students engaged in pair- or group-work tend to negotiate meaning more frequently than in teacher-student talk. They request confirmation, clarification, and otherwise modify their language to meet the needs of their conversation partner(s). As we have discussed before, the ability to negotiate meaning is not only a critical aspect of language use, it is also an important vehicle for improving language proficiency. Interaction is an essential element of language learning. As such, the need for interactive practice in the classroom suggests the following:

- ♨ Student-to-student interaction (such as pair/group work) should be planned as part of every class session.

- ♨ Students will find it beneficial to interact with a variety of partners. Teachers may find it helpful to have "assigned" partners for some activities and randomly selected partners for others.

- ♨ Pair/group tasks need to be carefully planned and managed so that students stay on task and in the foreign language. Students should know how they will be held accountable for the time spent working in pairs or groups. Time limits should be just long enough to get the job done but be short enough to avoid the enticement to use English.

- ♨ Tasks for pair/group work should provide for authentic interaction.

- ♨ It is not necessary for teachers to correct all errors. Nor should all errors be corrected immediately. Teachers can use observation of student errors to plan future instruction and practice.

Developing oral proficiency in a new language is a complex task. Students need to acquire extensive knowledge in a variety of areas and then be able to integrate their knowledge. Teachers can help students to develop skills in speaking a new language by providing rich, varied, and extensive opportunities to hear the language used in ways that allow for student internalization of language features. Classroom tasks should provide students with many changes to speak and to use the language in authentic ways, that is to communicate messages that have real purpose and meaning. Interaction with peers, in addition to interaction with the teachers, is critically important. Teachers will find students' speaking skills improve when extensive classroom time is allocated to student-to-student interactive tasks which require authentic, communicative language use. While research may not provide definitive answers as to how best to develop speaking skills, we do know more today than ever before about how people learn language in classroom settings. Using what we know may well help us to produce students who are successful language learners.

Bibliography

Adair-Hauck, B., R. Donato and P. Cumo. 1994. "Using a Whole Language Approach to Teach Grammar," in E. Glisan and J. Shrum, eds., *Teacher's Handbook. Contextualized Language Instruction*. Boston: Heinle and Heinle.

Asher, J. J. 1984. *Learning Another Language Through Actions: The Complete Teacher's Guidebook*. Los Gatos, CA: Sky Oaks Publications.

Canale, M. 1983. "From Communicative Competence to Communicative Language Pedagogy," in J. C. Richards and R. W. Schmidt, eds., *Language and Communication*. London: Longman.

Canale, M., and M. Swain. 1980. "Theoretical Bases of Communicative Approaches to Second Language Teaching and Testing." *Applied Linguistics* 1: 1-47.

Doughty, C. and T. Pica. 1986. "'Information Gap' Tasks: Do They Facilitate Second Language Acquisition?" *TESOL Quarterly* 20: 305-25.

Ellis, R. 1993. "The Structural Syllabus and Second Language Acquisition." *TESOL Quarterly* 27: 91-112.

Galloway, V. 1987. "From Defining to Developing Proficiency: A Look at the Decisions," in H. Byrnes and M. Canale, eds., *Defining and Developing Proficiency: Guidelines, Implementations, and Concepts*. Lincolnwood, IL: National Textbook.

Hendrickson, J. M. 1978. "Error Correction in Foreign Language Teaching: Recent Theory, Research, and Practice." *Modern Language Journal* 62: 387-425.

Johnson, D. W. and R. T. Johnson. 1989. *Cooperation and Competition: Theory and Research*. Edina, MN: Interaction Book.

Johnson, D. W. , R. T. Johnson, E. Johnson, and P. Roy. 1986. *Circles of Learning: Cooperation in the Classroom*. Revised edition. Alexandria, VA: Association for Supervision and Curriculum Development.

Kagan, S. 1992. *Cooperative Learning*. San Juan Capistrano, CA: Resource for Teachers.

Krashen, S. 1982. *Principles and Practice in Second Language Acquisition*. Oxford: Pergamon.

Larsen-Freeman, D. 1986. *Techniques and Principles in Language Teaching.* Oxford: Oxford University Press.

Long, M. H. 1983. "Native Speaker/Non-Native Speaker Conversation in the Second Language Classroom." In M. A. Clarke and J. Handscombe (eds.), *On TESOL '82.* Washington, DC: TESOL.

Long, M. H. and P. A. Porter. 1985. "Group Work, Interlanguage Talk, and Second Language Acquisition." *TESOL Quarterly* 19: 207-27.

Littlewood, W. 1981. *Communicative Language Teaching.* New York: Cambridge University Press.

Met, M. and V. Galloway. 1991. "Research in Foreign Language Curriculum," in P. Jackson, ed., *Handbook of Research on Curriculum.* New York: Macmillian.

Mings, R. C. 1993. "Changing Perspectives on the Utility of Error Correction in Second Language Acquisition." *Foreign Language Annals* 26: 171-79.

Nerenz, A. G., and C. K. Knop. 1982. "The Effect of Group Size on Students' Opportunity to Learn in the Second-Language Classroom," in A. Garfinkel, ed., *ESL and the Foreign Language Teacher.* Lincolnwood, IL: National Textbook.

Nunan, D. 1989. *Designing Tasks for the Communicative Classroom.* Cambridge: Cambridge University Press.

Nunan, D. 1991. "Communicative Tasks and the Language Curriculum." *TESOL Quarterly* 25: 279-95.

Omaggio Hadley, A. 1993. *Teaching Language in Context.* Boston: Heinle and Heinle.

Resnick, L. B. 1989. *Knowing, Learning, and Instruction: Essays in Honor of Robert Glaser.* Hillsdale, NJ: Lawrence Erlbaum Associates.

Richards, J. C. 1985. *The Context of Language Teaching.* Cambrige: Cambridge University Press.

Savignon, S. J. 1991. "Communicative Language Teaching: State of the Art." *TESOL Quarterly* 25: 261-77.

Shrum, J. and E. Glisan. 1994. *Teacher's Handbook. Contextualized Language Instruction.* Boston: Heinle and Heinle.

Slavin, R. E. 1983. *Cooperative Learning.* New York: Longman.

Swain, M. 1985. "Communicative Competence: Some Roles of Comprehensible Input and Comprehensible Output in its Development," in S. Gass and C. Madden, eds., *Input in Second Language Acquisition.* Rowley, MA: Newbury House.

chapter **8**

Writing

Virginia Scott
Vanderbilt University

QUESTION 1: **When should we begin to teach writing?**

Discussion

Most FL teachers would agree that listening, speaking, reading, and writing are all important skills. Traditionally, listening comprehension and speaking have been emphasized at the beginning level of FL study, and reading and writing have become increasingly more important at the intermediate and advanced levels. However, recent research in FL writing suggests that writing should be given more attention at all levels of FL study (Scott, 1992). While writing is frequently used as a support skill, expressive writing, or composition, is often given low priority in the FL curriculum. One reason for neglecting this kind of writing may be that students don't always know how to write in their native language, and teachers are overwhelmed by the challenge of teaching them to write in the target language. Another possible reason is that most of the theories that we have about teaching FL writing are borrowed from research in English and ESL, and classroom teachers do not have ready access to this information. Whatever the reason, we need to become more informed about the nature of FL writing and to focus more on writing in FL classes.

Students at all levels of language study use writing to practice newly learned words and structures. However, the kind of writing that involves arranging and linking words, sentences, and paragraphs is commonly either left for advanced-level students or neglected entirely. Research suggests that this kind of writing—composition—is both important and manageable for FL students regardless of their level (Scott, 1992).

Scholars in English describe writing as a dynamic activity during which the writer is engaged in a significant kind of thinking and discovery of meaning (Murray, 1980; Moxley, 1989). In a quest for meaning, the writer searches for ways to organize, synthesize, restate, and clarify. In the native language, the cognitive skills invoked by composing a narrative or descriptive text are complex but begin to emerge in very young children (Flower, 1988). In fact, many educators regard composition as a fundamental aspect of the learning process for students of any age.

Thus, students who begin to study a foreign language, regardless of their age, will have already developed some degree of writing competence in their native language. Research in ESL proposes that writing competence, or what a writer knows about writing, is not language-specific. Assumptions that students have about writing in their native language (L1) form the basis for new hypotheses about writing in a second language (L2) (Edelsky, 1982). Likewise, both good and poor writing strategies, such as planning, organizing, and revising, carry over from L1 to L2 (Zamel, 1983; Jones and Tetroe, 1987; Eisterhold, 1990; Friedlander, 1990).

It has also been recognized that a student's level of writing competence is not necessarily linked to grammatical competence (Krapels, 1990). A student who is capable of supplying correct answers on a grammar test in the target language may not necessarily be a competent writer in that language (Schultz, 1991). In fact, it has been proposed that students are able to express personal meaning in a foreign language before they have fully mastered basic linguistic structures (Scott, 1992).

QUESTION 2: What is the best way to teach students to write?

Discussion

Research suggests that students are capable of writing in the target language at any age or at any stage of the language learning process. However, students require direction, and the writing assignment is crucial to their success. Scott and Terry (1992) discuss a task-oriented approach which is founded on the idea that students at all levels need explicit guidelines in order to execute a writing assignment. They propose that each assignment consist of (1) a general **situation** followed by (2) a series of **tasks** that specify the language functions, vocabulary, and grammar structures necessary to complete the assignment. [See Appendix A.] The authors contend that these task-oriented writing assignments provide the organizational framework that helps students communicate a comprehensible, personalized message.

Using the same task-oriented approach, Scott (1992) proposes a developmental writing program designed to teach students to write compositions from the earliest stages of language study. In each composition assignment, the **situation** can remain the same for students at any stage of language learning, while the **tasks** can be modified to progress from simple to more complex language functions and structures. [See Appendix B.]

The challenge for FL teachers is clear: teach writing from the start! While students of all ages and all stages of language study will have varying levels of writing competence and grammatical knowledge, they can all benefit from the discovery that comes with composing a text in the target language.

QUESTION 3: What is the most effective way to teach writing as a process?

Discussion

Recently, much attention has been given to the notion that writing is a complex, non-linear process. This process, which begins from the moment a writer starts thinking about the topic to the moment the final text has been completed, involves using different kinds of strategies. Writers of all ages have developed writing strategies in their own language. Young, inexperienced writers may sit down and begin writing with little sense of where they are headed. Experienced writers may plan more extensively or may discover and create their meaning as they write. Many writers are unaware of how they go about writing, focusing their attention on the product or the text, rather than on the process or the strategies that they use to complete the writing task. Nevertheless, all writers use a variety of writing strategies, and no two writers compose alike.

Research in English composition provides much information about first-language writing. By analyzing writers in the act of writing, Flower and Hayes (1981) were able to propose a comprehensive model of the writing process. They divide composing into three main categories: **planning, translating,** and **reviewing. Planning** is described as the process of forming an internal, relatively abstract representation of the knowledge about the topic. Generating ideas, setting goals, and organizing are involved in this planning process. **Translating** is a term used to explain the process of putting images and ideas into language. **Reviewing** refers to the editing and revising that occurs throughout the entire writing process. Above all, Flower and Hayes (1981) emphasize that writing is a not a rigid sequence of set stages, but rather a process involving a set of options that can be used at any time during the act of writing.

While Flower and Hayes' (1981) model of the writing process is relevant to writing in both the native and the target language, certain aspects are more difficult when writing in the FL. The most challenging feature of the FL writing process is **generating ideas**. Every FL teacher has heard students say that they can't write because they don't know what to say. This source of frustration is potentially the largest stumbling block that students face when given a writing assignment. According to Scott (1992), the reason for this frustration is that students use L1 idea generation strategies when writing in the FL. That is, when students are assigned a writing topic in L1, they typically have ideas about what to say and then try to express those ideas in language. Similarly, with a FL writing assignment, students come up with elaborate ideas about the assigned topic and then try to transfer, or translate, those ideas directly into the FL. Since students are limited by a small lexicon and minimal grammatical knowledge, the end result is often incomprehensible.

In order to help students with idea generation in a FL, we should first encourage them to recall the words and expressions in the target language associated with the given topic. For example, in an essay on the importance of vacations, students should be guided to list specific words and expressions that come to mind and let those words shape their ideas. Second, the topic should be familiar and personal to the student writer. If the topic is culturally related, or somewhat unfamiliar, generating ideas will be more difficult since the writer will have less related knowledge stored in long-term memory (Caccamise, 1987). Finally, the writing assignment should provide enough direction to help students focus on the language of expression while generating ideas (Scott and Terry, 1992).

Another problematic aspect of the FL writing process is **reviewing**. The term **reviewing** refers to any kind of rereading and revising undertaken during the writing process. Since students often consider rereading to be an activity which occurs after the composition task has been completed, they must be taught to reread frequently while writing. Furthermore, they should be encouraged to read their texts aloud, either to themselves or to a classmate. Raimes (1987) suggests that rehearsing, or reading aloud, is an important FL composing strategy both for editing what is on the page and for generating new ideas.

Like rereading, revising should take place throughout the writing process. Students tend to regard revision primarily as the final editing stage of the writing process rather than an ongoing process of repair. Regardless of the language of expression, there are basically two kinds of revisions that a writer can make: (1) surface changes that do not alter the meaning, such as spelling, punctuation, tense, modality, additions, and deletions, and (2) content changes which alter the summary of the text, such as additions, deletions, and consolidations (Faigley and Witte, 1981). Typically, in the matter of FL writing, teachers and students readily engage in surface changes. The challenge, however, lies in teaching students to revise the content. Changes in the content often require direct suggestions from the teacher and can be incorporated in subsequent drafts.

In a study of revising strategies in L1 writing, Matsuhashi (1987) noted that the presence of the text played an important role in how students revised. Students who were asked to reread their essays, then put them aside and write five new things to be added to their texts, performed better than students who had their texts in front of them and were told to incorporate five new things. This type of strategy could be a good exercise for teaching FL students to alter or expand the content of their texts.

There is no clearly defined way of teaching the FL writing process. However, if students are taught that writing is not a linear think-write-rewrite process but rather a varied and dynamic process, they will be more likely to enjoy it. Furthermore, writing should not always be a solitary activity. Brainstorming for ideas, vocabulary, and language structures can be a class or group activity. Revising can be done either with a classmate or with the teacher. Ultimately, teachers as well as students will appreciate working on different aspects of the writing process rather than focusing only on the final text.

QUESTION 4: **In general, how important are grammar and spelling in writing?**

Discussion

We often assign compositions so that students can practice and reinforce linguistic structures. Accordingly, students usually view composition as another kind of grammar exercise. However, most current research on writing provides us with evidence that grammar and composition represent two different knowledge bases and that grammar study may have little to do with composing (Zamel, 1982). Research also suggests that inexperienced ESL and FL writers are focused on linguistic accuracy nearly to the point of obsession and give little attention to content and coherence. This research does not imply that we need to teach grammar and composition separately. Rather, it points to the importance of teaching students to differentiate between learning grammar and learning effective writing strategies. Finally, while most teachers would agree that grammar and spelling are important, we should avoid focusing so narrowly on accuracy before the final steps of the revising process.

QUESTION 5: Should students be allowed to translate from English to the target language?

Discussion

In most foreign language classrooms, students are strongly discouraged from translating, since they tend to translate verbatim from L1 to the FL. However, for many students, translation is the most "instinctive" and obvious strategy to use. While there is little or no empirical research on the use of translation as a FL writing strategy, we should address the issue directly and help students to develop alternative strategies, such as the ones suggested earlier.

QUESTION 6: How can students be encouraged to continue working on their writing skills at intermediate and advanced levels?

Discussion

Students will continue to work on their writing skills if they are appropriately challenged. The primary source of challenge comes from the **writing task**. Schultz (1991) proposes that the four traditional modes of discourse, namely description, narration, exposition, and argumentation, require different uses of language as well as different levels of cognitive processing. This researcher points out that beginning- and intermediate-level FL students practice primarily the descriptive and narrative modes, whereas advanced-level students are often assigned topics that require exposition and argumentation. Schultz argues that advanced-level students frequently show evidence of problems with expression and accuracy because they haven't learned to explain, define and analyze (exposition), or persuade and influence their intended audience (argumentation). For students in their third and fourth years of language study, the writing task should include expository and persuasive essays.

Scott (1992) believes that students should start at the earliest levels to practice writing descriptive, narrative, expository, and persuasive texts, so that these modes of discourse are familiar to them when they reach the advanced level of study in both language and literature. She describes a developmental writing program using task-oriented guidelines that directs students from the beginning stages of language study to use increasingly complex language and thought in all four modes of discourse. [See Appendix B.]

Omaggio Hadley (1993) describes writing tasks for advanced-level students that combine the use of narrative, descriptive, expository, and persuasive modes of discourse. A sample writing task illustrates how students can be guided to use several modes of discourse to write about personal life events: "What day was it? Where were you? Why do you remember the incident? What were you doing? Whom were you with? What happened? Why did it happen? What effect did the event have on you? What changed as a result of the action? (Omaggio Hadley, 1993: 334-35)." Omaggio Hadley's example of a writing task designed to guide students to analyze prose also requires students to use the four modes of discourse. Using *L 'Étranger* by Camus, she proposes the following questions:

> After reading the passage, what is the principal impression that you have of the nursing home and of its residents? How does Meursault (the principal character of the novel) see the nursing home and its residents? In creating his portrait of the nursing home, Camus uses a lot of striking images.... Analyze these aspects of the description.... Give a few details that show that Meursault has problems seeing or hearing the old people in the room. Give a few details that show that Meursault sees them as objects rather than as people. How does Meursault react emotionally? Give some examples from the text. Does Meursault understand the emotions of the old people in the room? Explain your response. (Omaggio Hadley, 1993: 337-338).

At intermediate and more advanced levels, writing tasks should challenge students to narrate, describe, explain, analyze, evaluate, support an opinion, and argue a viewpoint. Students are more likely to be motivated to work on their writing skills if the writing tasks go beyond asking for concrete facts and require them to explain and interpret events and ideas.

QUESTION 7: Are computers effective in teaching FL writing?

Discussion

Recently, there has been much interest in the effects of composing at the computer. While there is little concrete evidence available yet (see Pusack and Otto, this volume), research in L1 indicates that word processing is not just a writing tool, but also a teaching instrument which may affect the composing processes of student writers. Selfe (1986) states that in evaluating and developing computer programs for writing, teachers should consider:

  ◈   process problems such as planning and revising,

  ◈   attitude problems such as commitment and fear,

  ◈   mechanical problems such as spelling and agreement, and

  ◈   logic problems such as organizing sentences and paragraphs.

Most word processing programs support the mechanics of writing with subprograms such as a spell checker, a dictionary, and a thesaurus. However, there are new software programs that include data bases with lexical and grammatical information. Several such language-specific writing programs have been developed for teaching and learning FL writing. *Atajo* for Spanish (Dominguez, Noblitt, and Pet, 1994), *Quelle* for German (Kossuth, Noblitt, and Pet, 1995), and *système-D* for French (Noblitt, Pet, and Solá, 1992), are three noteworthy examples of software designed for FL writing. These programs provide rapid access to a bilingual dictionary, a verb conjugator, a grammar index, a vocabulary index, and a phrase index. No empirical data yet exist, however, regarding the effect that these programs have on the development of the foreign language learner's writing skills.

 While the FL writing software cited above can provide a new dimension to a high-school or college composition course, Greenia (1992) describes how teachers can use any word processing program to teach FL writing. According to his model, each student purchases a diskette on which the teacher has created a set of files. Some files are already full, such as the course description file and the file with samples of model texts. Most files are empty, such as the work in progress file (which may be designated as private space that the teacher promises not to inspect), the completed assignment file, a dialogue journal file, and a file for special exercises created by the teacher. His model encourages students to grapple with process problems, such as generating ideas through free writing, editing, and revising. He also includes many suggestions for increasing the volume of student writing, expanding the variety of writing assignments, and easing the teacher's grading load. Greenia, along with many FL teachers, is enthusiastic about the possibilities for using computers to teach writing.

QUESTION 8: How should writing be evaluated?

Discussion

When we evaluate student writing, our purpose is generally two-fold: (1) to help students improve their writing skills, and (2) to assess the quality of the writing (often in order to assign a grade). With regard to helping students improve their writing, opinions of educators differ. Lalande's (1982) study indicates that students are more likely to improve their writing when they correct their own work after the teacher has signaled the errors with error codes. Semke's (1984) study suggests that students benefit most from comments that focus primarily on the content. Barnett (1989) proposes giving feedback on both form and content and requiring students to rewrite their compositions two or three times. While there is no conclusive evidence regarding how teachers can help students improve their writing by responding to their written work, we should consider helping them improve their writing by evaluating their writing **process**. Given the importance of the recent focus on the process-nature of writing, we may want to begin thinking about devising ways to evaluate the strategies that students use to generate ideas, reread, and revise.

Just as there are several theories about how to help students improve their writing skills, there are different approaches to scoring written work. **Holistic scoring** involves assigning a single grade based on the overall impression of a whole text. **Analytical scoring** involves assigning separate grades to the various features of a composition, such as grammar, vocabulary, mechanics, fluency, and relevance (Terry, 1989). Another commonly used approach consists of giving two grades—one for **form** and one for **content**.

Assessing the quality of student writing and assigning a grade is often an important factor in motivating students. Chastain (1990) found that when students are assigned a grade for their written work, they are likely to write longer compositions with more complex sentences than when they are not being evaluated. However, he also found that there was no significant difference in the number of errors in compositions that were written for a grade and those that were not.

Finally, any system of evaluation that we adopt must conform to the theory about writing that we espouse. If we consider grammatical and lexical accuracy to be important, the evaluation system must assess those features of the student's text. If we are interested in a student's ideas, comprehensibility and coherence should be judged. If the writing process is considered to be as important as the final product, we should devise some way of evaluating how the student goes about the writing task.

Bibliography

Barnett, M. A. 1989. "Writing as Process." *The French Review* 63: 31-44.

Caccamise, D. J. 1987. "Idea Generation in Writing," in A. Matsuhashi, ed., *Writing in Real Time*. Norwood, NJ: Ablex.

Chastain, K. 1990. "Characteristics of Graded and Ungraded Compositions." *Modern Language Journal* 74: 10-14.

Dominguez, F., J. S. Noblitt and W. J. A. Pet. 1994. *Atajo*. Boston: Heinle and Heinle.

Edelsky, C. 1982. "Writing in a Bilingual Program: The Relation of L1 and L2 Texts." *TESOL Quarterly* 16: 211-28.

Eisterhold, J. C. 1990. "Reading-Writing Connections: Toward a Description for Second Language Learners," in B. Kroll ed., *Second Language Writing: Research Insights for the Classroom*. New York: Cambridge University Press.

Faigley, L. and S. Witte. 1981. "Analyzing Revision." *College Composition and Communication* 32: 400-14.

Flower, L. and J. R. Hayes. 1981. "A Cognitive Process Theory of Writing." *College Composition and Communication* 32: 365-87.

Flower, L. 1988. "The Construction of Purpose in Writing and Reading." *Occasional Paper 4*. Berkeley: Center for the Study of Writing.

Friedlander, A. 1990. "Composing in English: Effects of a First Language on Writing in English as a Second Language," in B. Kroll ed., *Second Language Writing: Research Insights for the Classroom*. New York: Cambridge University Press.

Greenia, G. D. 1992. "Computers and Teaching Composition in a Foreign Language." *Foreign Language Annals* 25: 33-46.

Hewins, C. 1986. "Writing in a Foreign Language: Motivation and the Process Approach." *Foreign Language Annals* 19: 219-23.

Jones, S. and J. Tetroe. 1987. "Composing in a Second Language," in A. Matsuhashi, ed., *Writing in Real Time*. Norwood, NJ: Ablex.

Kossuth, K., J. S. Noblitt and W. J. A. Pet. 1995. *Quelle*. Boston: Heinle and Heinle.

Krapels, A.R. 1990. "An Overview of Second Language Writing Process Research," in B. Kroll ed., *Second Language Writing: Research Insights for the Classroom*. New York: Cambridge University Press.

Kroll, B., ed. 1990. *Second Language Writing: Research Insights for the Classroom*. New York: Cambridge University Press.

Lalande, J. 1982. "Reducing Composition Errors: An Experiment." *Modern Language Journal* 66: 140-49.

Matsuhashi, A. 1987. "Revising the Plan and Altering the Text," in A. Matsuhashi, ed., *Writing in Real Time*. Norwood, NJ: Ablex.

Moxley, J. M. 1989. "Tearing Down the Walls: Engaging the Imagination," in J. M. Moxley, ed., *Creative Writing in America: Theory and Pedagogy*. Urbana, IL: National Council of Teachers of English.

Murray, D. M. 1980. "Writing as Process: How Writing Finds Its Own Meaning," in T. R. Donovan and B. W. McClelland eds., *Eight Approaches to Teaching Composition*. Urbana, IL: National Council of Teachers of English.

Noblitt, J. S., W. J. A. Pet and D. Solá. 1992. *système-D*. Boston: Heinle & Heinle.

Omaggio Hadley, A. C. 1993. *Teaching Language in Context*. 2nd ed. Boston: Heinle & Heinle.

Raimes, A. 1987. "Language Proficiency, Writing Ability, and Composing Strategies: A Study of ESL College Student Writers." *Language Learning* 37: 439-67.

Schultz, J. M. 1991. "Writing Mode in the Articulation of Language and Literature Classes: Theory and Practice." *Modern Language Journal* 75: 411-17.

Schultz, J. M. 1990. "Mapping and Cognitive Development in the Teaching of Foreign Language Writing." *The French Review* 64: 978-88.

Selfe, C. L. 1986. *Computer-Assisted Instruction in Composition*. Urbana, IL: National Council of Teachers of English.

Semke, H. D. 1984. "The Effects of the Red Pen." *Foreign Language Annals* 17: 195-202.

Scott, V. M. 1992. "Write From the Start: A Task-Oriented Developmental Writing Program for Foreign Language Students," in R. Terry, ed., *Dimension: Language '91 Making a World of Difference*. Valdosta, GA: Southern Conference on Language Teaching.

Scott, V. M. and R. M. Terry. 1992. *système-D Teacher's Guide*. Boston: Heinle & Heinle.

Terry, R. M. 1989. "Teaching and Evaluating Writing as a Communicative Skill." *Foreign Language Annals* 22: 43-52.

Zamel, V. 1983. "The Composing Processes of Advanced ESL Students: Six Case Studies." *TESOL Quarterly* 17: 167-87.

Zamel, V. 1982. "Writing: The Process of Discovering Meaning." *TESOL Quarterly* 16: 195-209.

Appendix A

Situation: **You have been asked to write a complete description of yourself for the new student files.**

Tasks:
1) Describe yourself physically.
     Function: Describing people
     Grammar: Adjective position and agreement
     Vocabulary: Hair colors, body, face

2) Describe your personality, indicating positive as well as negative traits.
     Grammar: Negation
     Vocabulary: Personality

3) Conclude with a statement about how you feel about your school.
     Function: Expressing an opinion.

(Modified from Scott and Terry, 1992, p. 25).

Appendix B

Situation: You have heard that American and French students are different. In order to promote cultural understanding, you are writing an article for a French magazine about American students.

First-year tasks:
1) Begin with a general remark about American students.
2) Describe the way a female student might look.
3) Describe the way a male student might look.
4) Indicate three things that some American students like to do.
5) Conclude with a personal opinion about American students.

Second-year tasks:
1) Begin with a general remark about American students.
2) Describe the way students, both male and female, might look.
3) Indicate at least five things that some American students like to do, and three things that they don't like to do.
4) Conclude with several personal opinions about the individuality or conformity of American students.

Third-year tasks:
1) You will argue either for or against the idea that all American students are alike. Begin with a thesis statement.
2) Describe American students.
3) Define the term "stereotype" as it relates to American students.
4) Conclude by showing how the argument supports the thesis statement.

(Modified from Scott, 1992, pages 7-8.)

chapter 9

Grammar

L. Kathy Heilenman
The University of Iowa

QUESTION 1: Do we know what effect grammar instruction has on proficiency?

Discussion

One of the yet unresolvable questions in foreign language teaching concerns the effect of explicit grammar instruction on students' eventual level of proficiency in the target language (see, for example, Kelly, 1976). The question of explicit grammar instruction, as Yip (1994) has pointed out, is far from simple, and the issues involved are many and complex. Moreover, the research literature is extensive, and within the space of this chapter only a small sample of the studies available can be discussed. Readers wishing further information are referred to the many discussions of this topic available elsewhere (e.g., Lightbown, 1985; Rutherford, 1987; Long, 1988; Rutherford and Sharwood Smith, 1988; Larsen-Freeman, 1989; Ellis, 1990; Larsen-Freeman, 1991b; Larsen-Freeman and Long, 1991; VanPatten, 1992a, 1992b; Heafford, 1993; Pica 1994). It is important, however, for teachers and other practitioners to become aware of the limitations as well as the benefits of scientific research into second language acquisition.

QUESTION 2: Why don't learners learn the grammar rules they are taught?

Discussion

Any attempt to answer this question involves looking at both sides of the equation: what learners learn and what teachers teach. To begin with the latter, a consideration of what we mean by the term **grammar** is helpful. There are two issues: 1) the extent to which the grammar presented by teachers and textbooks is an accurate representation of the language native speakers use; and 2) the extent to which any collection of explicit grammar rules reflects the internalized system used in the comprehension and production of language.

DiVito (1991), for French, and Glisan and Drescher (1993), for Spanish, have recently studied extensive corpora of native-speaker speech and writing. They found that many traditional grammar points are represented only infrequently in actual use, while others that are quite frequent receive little coverage. Double object pronouns (the use of two pronouns, as in "She gave him it," for example) are quite rare in both the French and Spanish corpora studied, but are usually accorded quite a bit of explanatory space in textbooks. It may simply be impractical, then, to expect beginning and even intermediate students to master aspects of the target language that are rarely used. Further, such rarity of use may reflect psycholinguistic or discourse constraints that, although only very poorly understood at present, may make it difficult for learners to master the "rules" dealing with infrequent structures. This possibility leads us directly to the second point, the psychological reality of grammar rules. As DiPietro (1985) has put it, grammar "is a statement of language as an artifact" (p. 499); it is not a direct representation of the processes underlying language use. Along the same lines, Westney (1994) provides a detailed analysis of "rules"—what they should look like and how they work—and claims that all rules are compromises between the demands of generalization (how many language facts one rule can account for), vague terminology (the use of terms such as "completeness" and "incompleteness" to explain the difference in use between progressive and simple tenses in English), and the underlying complexity of language (rules only imperfectly reflect linguistic reality). He concludes that there is no obvious, best description of a language and that both learners and teachers should assume "a cautious, if not skeptical, attitude towards any pedagogical treatment of language regularities" (p. 73).

In a similar vein, Eubank and Beck (1993) point out that current linguistic thought as reflected in Chomsky's Government and Binding Theory of Universal Grammar (UG) (Chomsky, 1981) has largely done away with a rule-based format, using instead a more abstract characterization of language as composed of innate, specific principles and parameters. These principles and parameters involve very complex clusters of language characteristics that bear little resemblance to traditional grammar rules and that are, in fact, assumed to be unlearnable/unteachable in the sense of school learning. In addition, within this perspective, first language acquisition is seen as a "triggering" process wherein certain input data set "parameters" to certain settings, which in turn determine various language-specific properties. To give only one example, the "pro-drop" parameter can be said to group such disparate constructions as the presence or absence of pronoun subjects and pleonastic pronouns (e.g., the "it" in sentences such as in "It is raining"), as well as verb endings (e.g., White 1989).

The assumption, then, is that input containing one member of the cluster (say subject pronouns) will set the pro-drop parameter to either "plus" or "minus" (in this case, it would be set to minus) which, in turn, will cause the other members of the cluster to be acquired. Within this framework, then, the learning of syntax is seen as developmental and unconscious rather than a function of the conscious learning and practicing of rules. As a result, the interesting question for second language acquisition theory is whether or not adult L2 learners have access to UG, either directly or indirectly, through their L1 or, if they are required to learn the L2 using non-language-specific cognitive and problem solving strategies, as in Krashen's (1991) postulated conscious learning monitor or Schwartz' (1993) learned linguistic knowledge. This brief summary can only give the flavor of what is a very complex area of endeavor. Interested readers should consult sources such as Cook (1988, 1994), White (1989), and Eubank and Beck (1993) for further information. It should also be emphasized that Universal Grammar is not the only linguistic theory to eschew a rule-based approach to learning.

Researchers working within a cognitive approach that assumes no innate language acquisition device have also suggested that rules, especially morphological rules such as those governing irregular verbs or adjective endings, represent one way of describing a language (e.g., MacWhinney, Leinbach, et al., 1989; Bybee 1991). These rules do not, however, represent the way in which that language is accessed or produced, nor do they reflect the processes first and second language learners go through as they learn the language. Instead, the suggestion is that learners gradually build up words or exemplars of the various forms and establish connections between them. The resultant system can be described using paradigms and verb charts, but the language itself is not the same thing as those paradigms and charts. Again, this is an oversimplified account of a complex area of research in both linguistics and psychology, and readers are urged to consult sources such as Hatch and Yoshitomi (1993) for more information.

Several studies support the position that language learning is not the simple aggregation of structures represented by a typical grammatical syllabus. Larsen-Freeman and Long (1991) summarize research indicating that grammatical structures emerge only slowly and imperfectly in learners' interlanguages (an interlanguage is usually defined as a transitional linguistic system characteristic of second language learners). This, of course, is in direct contradiction to the linear, building-block-like order of most textbook grammar presentations. In a series of research reports, Pienemann and his colleagues (Pienemann 1984a, 1984b; Clahsen and Muysken 1986) have shown that learners of German as a second language pass through developmental stages as they acquire German word order. Moreover, these stages appear to be constrained by learners' ability to process the language to which they are exposed and learners appear impervious to instructional intervention that is not in sync with their acquisition stage. Instruction in Stage 4, for example, will affect learners at Stage 3, but will have no effect on learners at Stages 1 or 2. This research has led to the conclusion that form-focused instruction (not necessarily the teaching of "rules") can be useful in second language learning, but only if such instruction operates within certain psycholinguistic constraints. Similar developmental or acquisitional orders have also been found for subsystems in various languages. [See Larsen-Freeman and Long, 1991; VanPatten, 1992a, 1992b for discussion.]

An additional line of research may also throw some light on the question of why learners don't seem to learn what they're taught. Green and Hecht (1992) investigated the extent to which 300 German students at various levels of English learning were able to correct errors and state the rule they believed applied. Results indicated that, as a group, the German students were able to achieve 78% of the possible corrections but were able to produce an "acceptable" rule in only 46% of the cases. Further, although it was the case that being able to articulate a correct rule was related to producing an appropriate correction, the reverse was not true. In 70% of the cases where learners gave an incorrect rule and in 55% of the cases where they gave no rule at all, learners were still able to provide an appropriate correction. Green and Hecht conclude that a balance needs to be found between the classroom time devoted to explicit rule learning and that given to communicative activities, especially in light of the fact that not all rules are equally easy to remember or learn. It should be noted that an alternative interpretation of these results might be that learners were originally helped by learning the rules but that they no longer needed to use them (the rules had been internalized, so to speak), and thus were no longer able to articulate them. Although this internalization is possible, it is very difficult, as the authors point out, to untangle the effects of length of exposure and type of rule-based instruction provided for their subjects. There is, moreover, no clear indication that more advanced learners (in terms of time) were less able to articulate the rules than were beginning or intermediate learners.

In summary, then, learners do **not** tend to learn what they are taught under two conditions: (1) when the "rules" do not reflect psycholinguistic processes and (2) when learners are not yet ready to acquire the target structures. Moreover, there is evidence that language knowledge, as represented by the ability to articulate grammar rules, may be independent of the ability to produce correct language. To give only one additional example, Heilenman and McDonald (McDonald and Heilenman, 1992; Heilenman and McDonald, 1993) have shown that English-speaking classroom learners of French listening to French sentences are able to abandon an English-based sentence interpretation strategy almost immediately but, at the same time, are unable to effectively use strategies requiring the processing of pronouns and verb endings until they reach the third year of college-level instruction. Thus, learners have learned something not taught (the word order strategy) but prove unable to use something (pronouns and verb endings) to which a substantial amount of instructional time had been devoted.

QUESTION 3: **Should teachers provide explicit grammar instruction or are learners best served by a classroom atmosphere that encourages "picking up" the language through teacher provision of rich, contextualized input?**

Discussion

As might be expected, given the previous discussion, the evidence here is mixed and often contradictory. Ellis (1990), for example, has summarized the relevant research, reaching the conclusion that, overall, formal instruction does indeed contribute to successful second language learning. Similarly, Odlin (1994), discussing a series of articles on pedagogical grammar, has also concluded that instruction makes a positive difference. These researchers would seem to imply that teachers should provide explicit grammar instruction. On the other hand, Krashen and Terrell (1983) suggest the limitations of grammar teaching, stating that "any grammar-based method which purports to develop communication skills will fail with the majority of students" (p. 16). They posit, instead, that comprehensible input (input that contains language not yet acquired but which the learner is ready to acquire), when combined with learner openness to the input (low affective filter), constitutes both a necessary and sufficient condition for successful second language learning (Krashen, 1991). In a similar vein, Eubank and Beck (1993), reviewing the research literature in the area of Universal Grammar, have concluded that formal, explicit instruction and practice have only a short-term effect on the language behavior of second language learners.

A closer look at four recent studies investigating the effect of explicit grammar instruction sheds some light on why the question of the efficacy of explicit grammar instruction in the classroom is so difficult to prove or disprove. Scott (1989, 1990) studied the performance of college-level learners of French under two conditions: (1) **explicit** (presentation of rules plus model sentences) and (2) **implicit** (structures were embedded in stories and students were asked to answer content questions and "notice" the structures targeted). The measure used was a discrete-point type, fill-in-the-blank test that focused on accuracy of use. The structures targeted were pronouns and the subjunctive.

In both studies, after controlling for prior knowledge via a pre-test, learners who had received explicit instruction showed greater gains than did those who had received implicit instruction. These results are difficult to interpret, however. Essentially, Scott has shown that learners who received explicit, rule-based instruction on two grammatical structures were better able to fill in blanks and respond to multiple-choice, short answer questions in the absence of context. Although such explicit instruction may indeed provide students with higher test scores (assuming that the measure used here is similar to many classroom grammar tests), it cannot be assumed that the knowledge permitting the explicit groups to outperform the implicit groups would automatically transfer to other areas (e.g., free conversation, listening comprehension, etc).

Further, as Krashen (1991) points out, it is likely that both structures were beyond the students' capacity to acquire via input (implicit instruction). In other words, one way of interpreting these results is that students in the explicit conditions outperformed those in the implicit conditions because they were able to apply conscious knowledge presumably gained during explicit grammar instruction to a test that rewarded that type of knowledge. These studies, then, indicate that if the ability to successfully complete discrete-point, form-focused tests is an instructional goal, then explicit, rule-based instruction (at least for the structures studied) is probably more effective than simply exposing students to examples, even extensive examples, of the structure under consideration, at least in the short term.

Another study (Master, 1994), investigated the effect of systematic instruction on the English article system in regard to the performance of ESL university-level students enrolled in courses focusing on the development of academic writing skills. Master provided six hours of instruction on article usage for the experimental group, with the control group receiving no such instruction. Both groups made gains (calculated from the administration of a 58-item fill-in-the blank test at the beginning and end of a ten-week period). The experimental group showed statistically significant gains in correct article usage, whereas the control group (which received no additional instruction) did not. Master (1994) reports a replication of this study with similar results, which he interprets as showing the effect of systematic instruction on the speed of acquisition "by making students aware of and increasing their conscious control of the way the article system works" (p. 247).

Again, however, extension of these results to a blanket endorsement of explicit grammar instruction should be made with caution. The learners involved were relatively advanced and may have been able to take advantage of the instruction provided in order to fine tune their production of articles. There is no guarantee that similar results would occur with beginning or intermediate learners. A final caveat concerning the importation of these results into the classroom comes from an inspection of the practical significance of the gains made by students in relationship to the time expended. In effect, students in Master's experimental condition went from an average score of 77% correct to an average score of 83% correct (a gain of 6 percentage points), with those in the control condition going from an average score of 76% correct to an average score of 78% correct (a gain of 2 percentage points). Research can tell us that this difference is statistically significant; that is, that the results obtained were not obtained by chance. It cannot, however, make the decision either as to cost-effectiveness or as to substantive, practical significance in individual classrooms.

A fourth study (Doughty, 1991) investigated the role of instruction in the learning of relativization (relative clauses) in English. This subsystem of English was chosen because previous work had already delineated many of the parameters along which research design decisions could be made. Three different hypotheses predicting order of acquisition were available, with previous second language acquisition research indicating that markedness plays a role in acquisition. More specifically, the projection model proposed by Zobl (1985) could be used to predict learner behavior. This model suggests that when a group of structures are related implicationally so that the acquisition of one implies the acquisition of all others below it in a chain, acquisition of the most marked (least frequent, most complex) structure will automatically trigger acquisition of the rest of the chain. That is, English relative clauses in which the relative pronoun functions as the subject of the clause (examples from Doughty, 1991) ("The girl who was sick went home") are the least marked and thus the easiest to acquire, followed by relative pronouns marking the direct object ("The girl whom I saw was pretty"), then the indirect object ("The girl whom I gave the present to was absent"), object of a preposition ("I found the book that John was talking about"), possessive ("I know the girl whose father died"), and finally, object of a comparison ("The person who John is taller than is Mary").

The projection model predicts that presenting the more complex structures to learners will help them profit from the markedness condition so that structures further down the chain will be learned without overt presentation. Subjects were 20 international students at the middle levels of proficiency in an intensive ESL program in the United States. Extensive pretesting determined that prior ability to deal with relative clauses was minimal. Subjects were divided into three groups: a control group, which was exposed to relative clauses with no instruction in relativization; and two experimental groups, each of which received instructional treatments via computer in addition to exposure. In addition, baseline data on all tasks were collected from native speakers of English. As part of a reading lesson, all groups were presented with material containing examples of object-of-a-preposition relative clauses. One experimental group received meaning-oriented instruction (lexical and semantic rephrasings and sentence rephrasings), while the other received a rule-oriented treatment (instruction on relativization through explicit rules and sentence manipulation). The control group was simply exposed to the relevant sentences (all groups spent an equal amount of time completing the material). As was the case with the studies described above, gain scores (post-test minus pre-test) were computed, with both experimental groups clearly outperforming the control group and with the meaning-oriented group slightly outperforming the rule-oriented group. In addition, marked relativization (object of a preposition only was taught) was found to generalize to other relativization contexts.

Finally, only the meaning-oriented group demonstrated substantial comprehension of the texts used in the materials. In other words, those subjects who received meaning-oriented instruction performed as well as those receiving rule-oriented instruction while at the same time producing superior comprehension scores (tasks were answering questions and writing a recall summary in the native language). In her discussion of the results, Doughty was able to refer to the actual form of instruction since all treatment sessions were available for replay on the computer. She suggests that the results obtained were a function of the explicitness of the presentations (subjects' attention was drawn to the relative clauses in the two instructional conditions) and of perceptual saliency (the capturing of subjects' attention by computer highlighting and capitalization of relevant material on the screen). Since both experimental groups produced roughly equivalent gain scores, she further suggests that metalinguistic rule statement (the rule-oriented group) does not make a difference.

Again, however, questions remain and the story is only partially told. As Doughty points out, the long-term effects of instruction were not addressed and improvement may well have been temporary. Second, although there is evidence that teaching more marked forms, with the expectation that less marked forms will also be acquired is effective, we have no insight into why and how this phenomenon might occur. Further, Hamilton (1994) has recently produced evidence that modifies this claim, indicating that the generalization to less marked forms is limited to levels immediately above learners' current levels. Finally, as is frequently the case with empirical studies of second language acquisition, implications for actual classroom use are elusive. The concept of markedness is notoriously slippery, with much disagreement as to how marked versus unmarked forms should be defined in other areas of language (see, for example White, 1989). Further, even if we could define all of language X in terms of marked-to-unmarked implicational sequences, we might well find that these sequences, taken together, interact to further complicate matters.

In summary, the studies discussed above, when taken in conjunction with many others (see studies listed in Question 1), indicate that explicit grammar instruction seems to be helpful for some tasks, for some learners, some of the time. Instruction does not seem to change the course of development in any important manner, but it may well accelerate the development of second language proficiency, at least in the short term and in certain areas of language. We do not have clear answers as to the effect of explicit grammar instruction in the long term, nor do we know much about how explicit grammar instruction interacts with the acquisition of other aspects of communicative competence, such as vocabulary acquisition, discourse structure, pronunciation, and so on (Hatch and Yoshitomi, 1993; Odlin, 1994).

QUESTION 4:   If learners' errors aren't corrected, won't their language fossilize?

Discussion

Higgs and Clifford (1982) have described a class of foreign/second language learners they have labeled as "terminal 2/2+." These learners were apparently "stuck" at the Advanced/Advanced-Plus level of speaking on the ACTFL proficiency scale. That is, they exhibited "fossilized" language behavior that they were apparently unable to ameliorate. Higgs and Clifford attribute this phenomenon to the learners' having arrived at the 2/2+ level through "communication-first" experience—either in a classroom where grammatical precision was not valued or through learning the language in a natural, uninstructed setting. They compare these terminal learners to others who have arrived at the same point through an "accuracy-first" program and who, apparently, were capable of progressing beyond the 2/2+ boundary (the 2/2+ level is described as being able to "fully participate in casual conversation, express facts, give instructions, describe, report on, and provide narration about current, past, and future activities").

Although Higgs and Clifford recognize that the attainment of the 2/2+ level represents a substantial achievement for classroom learners, they nevertheless suggest that it is professionally unethical, as they put it, to "condemn the student-client to a proficiency level far below the one to which he or she aspires" (p. 75). Leaving aside the issue of whether language programs should be organized for the majority of students (those for whom a 2/2+ rating would represent a quite satisfactory, even admirable achievement), or for the minority (those students who do eventually continue to quite advanced levels of proficiency), let us examine Higgs and Clifford's description of "terminal 2s" from the point of view of research design. In essence, the data they present are limited, anecdotal and, at best, suggestive. These data in no way prove or even imply that accuracy-based, explicit instruction is necessary in order to avoid producing students whose progress is permanently halted at a certain level. In the first place, we cannot tell if these learners have really ceased to progress, or if they are simply in the middle of a "plateau phase" (VanPatten, 1988). Further, and in a real sense, what we have here are not "data," but "stories" about learners within a certain context (the CIA language school), who appear to have ceased progress at a certain level.

Counter evidence in the sense of stories from other contexts is also available. The majority of teachers, for example, can also describe learners who appear to have ceased to make progress, in spite of massive provision of grammar- and accuracy-based instruction. In both cases, however, we are unable to assess the evidence as to why progress has halted or even if progress has, in truth, come to a standstill. We can hypothesize based on our own experience (which is essentially what Higgs and Clifford have done), but that is all. This is an area where further research, perhaps of the type called for by Higgs and Clifford themselves, is definitely in order.

The issue of correction, however, deserves further discussion. Given that both teachers and learners seem to feel the necessity for such correction, it is worthwhile asking if it helps, and if so, how. DeKeyser (1993) has reviewed the studies available in this area, concluding that (1) there are very few such studies and (2) the results provide little support one way or the other. There are, of course, reasons for this lacuna. Before we ask if correction helps, we have to define what we mean by correction. We also have to ask if correction helps differently at different linguistic stages, for different linguistic structures, for different age groups, and for different students. DeKeyser (1993) presents the results of a classroom study comparing two groups of Dutch learners of French in the Dutch-speaking part of Belgium. The teacher in one group was asked to correct mistakes as frequently and as explicitly as possible, while the other teacher was asked to avoid correction. The treatment period was an entire school year, and testing instruments included an aptitude measure (grammatical sensitivity), a measure of motivation, a measure of anxiety, three oral communication tasks (interview, picture description, and story telling), and a grammatical achievement test (60 fill-in-the-blank items targeting six problems of French grammar). DeKeyser audiotaped and transcribed ten class periods and found that in the error-correction class, correction was quite explicit, while in the other class, although there was a good deal of teacher restatement of correct forms, there was no direct, explicit correction of student errors.

His results indicated that, overall, error correction did not lead to an improvement in second language performance. The entire set of results is complex, but a few findings are of interest. As already stated, error correction did not seem to affect either proficiency, as measured by the three oral communication tasks, or achievement, as measured by the grammar test. Nevertheless, error correction during oral communicative activities interacted with individual difference variables in various ways. For example, students with low anxiety did better on a written grammar test after systematic error correction. Students with high extrinsic motivation (as measured by a 5-item scale with questions such as "I find it important to get good grades for French this year") did better without error correction on measures of oral accuracy and fluency.

Once more, we are left with as many questions as answers. The issue of whether or not error correction is effective is simply too broad. In all likelihood, error correction of certain kinds may be effective with certain learners in certain situations. Separate lines of research address these issues. Two studies (Tomasello and Herron, 1988; 1989) have indicated that corrective feedback is more effective if learners are allowed to develop a hypothesis and then receive feedback, thus allowing them to make a comparison and to correct their initial analysis. In Tomasello and Herron (1989), for example, college-level English-speaking students of French were first allowed to "go down the garden path" of a potential generalization (e.g., that the verb *savoir*, "to know something as a fact," could be extended to "being acquainted with someone," *connaître*). Students were presented with three sentences to translate, all of which verified the hypothesis that the French verb *savoir* covered the same lexical territory as the English verb "to know." Students were than asked to translate a fourth sentence, one in which their initial hypothesis would be falsified. After they had produced the incorrect equivalent, they were informed that it was incorrect and were given the correct answer. The control group was simply presented with all four sentences at once, with the teacher indicating that the fourth sentence would be different from the others.

Results of a translation test given later indicated that students in the "garden path" condition performed significantly better than did the control group students on this item. Again, although these results are suggestive, they do not provide direct methodological guidance for teachers. We simply cannot say that all feedback, or even the majority of such feedback, should be of the "garden path" variety. At best, teachers can add this type of activity to their repertoire of correction techniques, with the awareness that there may be a significant effect for certain students, on certain structures, using a certain task. We cannot simply assume that it would be effective for all students, on all structures, using different types of tasks.

Another study investigating negative student feedback was conducted by Carroll and Swain (1993). This study with 100 adult Spanish-speaking learners of ESL at the low-intermediate level, examined negative feedback on dative alternation with verbs both permitting and blocking this structural change (e.g., "Ken made a bookcase for his son/Ken made his son a bookcase" versus "We ordered pizza for all the students/ *We ordered all the students pizza." [* indicates an ungrammatical sentence]). There were five conditions:

- ♦ learners received explicit grammar-rule information when they made a mistake
- ♦ learners were simply told their response was wrong
- ♦ learners were corrected by being provided with a model of the correct response
- ♦ learners were asked "if they were sure" when they made an error
- ♦ learners were given no feedback.

Results indicated that the provision of explicit grammar rule information was the most beneficial and that, overall, all groups receiving feedback outperformed the group that received none. As Carroll and Swain point out, however, it is difficult to generalize these results to the classroom, given that the experiment was laboratory- rather than classroom-based, the time between learning and testing was short (one week), and only one, rather formal task (transforming one dative version to the other where appropriate) was used. In addition, Carroll and Swain did not control for time on task, and the most beneficial condition—provision of grammar rule information—also provided learners the most time.

A final area of research with implications for classroom practice is that concerning the question of "ultimate attainment." Essentially, this research asks if second language learners can ever attain the same level of proficiency as native speakers. In general, and with a few exceptions, for learners who begin the study of their second language as adults, the answer has been no. In fact, as Selinker (1992: 251) has put it, "non-learning" or fossilization is a persistent problem in second language acquisition, and the cessation of learning, often at a point quite distant from target language norms, is more the rule than it is the exception.

Debate continues within this area, with various factors being implicated (e.g., social and psychological factors, age, lack of access to UG, etc.). Several researchers argue quite convincingly that attention to form is important for eventual attainment. Ioup, Boustagui, El Tigi, and Moselle (1994), for example, studied two female adult learners of Egyptian Arabic, both with extensive residence in Cairo. One of the learners had never received formal instruction; the other had received extensive formal instruction. Testing revealed that both women had attained levels of proficiency virtually indistinguishable from that of native speakers. The researchers attempted to account for the success of the untutored learner by reference to her attention to form (she paid attention, for example, to language forms, and found it important to master grammar). Nevertheless, it seems quite unlikely that this subject's unusual success in all aspects, including the social and pragmatic, was due to attention to form alone, particularly since she had never received explicit instruction. They further speculate that a few individuals are simply exceptionally talented language learners.

Another study (Sorace, 1993) looked at the internalized grammars of French- and English-speaking L2 learners of Italian. Results indicated that there were two different ways of being "near-native": **incompleteness** (the grammar lacks items found in native speaker grammar) and **divergence** (the grammar differs from native speaker grammar). Sorace further suggests that these competence differences reflect L1 differences. A final comment in this area comes from Cook (1994), who points out that someone with two languages is not really comparable to two people with one language each, and that any attempt to make such a comparison is logically flawed. In other words, the eventual goal of L2 teaching, it is suggested, is not the theoretical monolingual native speaker, but rather the competent user of two (or more) languages. From this perspective, the issue of incomplete learning or fossilization is put into a more realistic perspective, one that permits "deviance" from monolingual norms in the service of a bilingual (or trilingual) competence that will vary according to sociological and psychological needs.

QUESTION 5:   What role can grammar play in foreign/second language teaching and learning?

Discussion

Ellis (1990; 1993), after reviewing much of the research in second language acquisition as it relates to teaching, has concluded that the one lesson that should have been learned is that of the insufficiency of a simple model that equates input with output. That is, learners, rather than teachers and textbooks, are the ultimate source of control in language learning, and the relationship between what is taught and what is learned is indirect at best. Further, what Ellis (1993) calls the PPP (present, practice, and more practice) approach to language teaching appears to be ineffective in producing the results desired. What is needed, then, is not a return to the model that assumes a grammar structure presented should be a grammar structure mastered, but rather a rethinking of the place of grammar within communicative language teaching.

As many researchers suggest, we need instruction that allows learners to focus on form within a communicative context (Rutherford, 1987; Rutherford and Sharwood Smith, 1988; Ellis, 1993; Harley, 1993; Sharwood Smith, 1993; Spada and Lightbown, 1993; VanPatten and Cadierno, 1993; and Kumaravadivelu, 1994). Such activities would not represent a return to isolated grammar teaching, nor would they imply that student output be restricted. Instead, emphasis needs to be placed on helping students "notice" language forms that might not be in focus within a meaning-based curriculum. This type of "consciousness-raising" or "enhanced input" activity differs radically from the more traditional present-practice-more practice, form-focused communication activities where learners' attention is focused on language as preparation for a later, more communicative phase. Instead, activities are designed that allow learners to focus on language form without necessarily implying any immediate production of that form. Indeed, as Fotos (1993) points out, the assumption is that there will be a gap of indeterminate length between "noticing" and "acquiring." Examples of these types of activities are provided by Day and Shapson (1991), Fotos (1993), and VanPatten (1993a, 1993b), among others. VanPatten (1993b) suggests the following guidelines:

- teach only one thing at a time
- keep meaning in focus
- learners must 'do something' with the input
- use both oral and written input
- move from sentences to connected discourse
- keep the psycholinguistic processing mechanisms in mind

(pp.438-439).

Noticing forms is important, since many of the linguistic features learners have difficulty with may fall into one or more of the following categories: 1) they may be non-salient or hard to notice, as in the case of direct object pronouns in French; 2) they may be infrequent in the input, as is the case with conditional forms in French in immersion classrooms (Day and Shapson, 1991); or 3) they may simply be unnecessary for successful top-down (getting-the-gist-type) comprehension, as in the case of the majority of inflectional endings (MacWhinney, 1992). Thus, in theory, if activities can be devised which require or facilitate learners' noticing of such items, then, theoretically, their learning will be more effective. Several terms have been suggested for these types of activities. Rutherford and Sharwood Smith (1988), for example, discuss the term "consciousness-raising" which they define as "the deliberate attempt to draw the learner's attention specifically to the formal properties of the target language" (p. 274). Sharwood Smith (1993) has since termed this "input enhancement," pointing out the many forms and degrees of elaboration and explicitness such enhancement can take (Sharwood Smith, 1990). The "garden path" studies (Tomasello and Herron 1988; 1989) referred to earlier, for example, can be seen as examples of providing enhanced input.

Another role for a focus on form is suggested by classroom-based studies that have attempted to investigate the utility of providing enhanced input, both initially and as a means of helping learners notice their own deviations from target language norms. As might be expected, the results are mixed, partially, no doubt, because of the difficulties inherent in conducting such studies. The working definition of a term such as "noticing" is far from evident, and the same problems seen in other areas are seen here (e.g., generalizability to other learning situations, validity of the task(s) used to measure language gain, and so forth). Day and Shapson (1991) studied the effect of providing materials focusing on the conditional tense with seventh graders in French immersion classes. Unlike a similar study (Harley 1989) focusing on the preterit/ imperfect distinction and using slightly younger learners (grade 6), Day and Shapson found positive, long-term benefits from the five- to six-week curriculum unit. It is, however, impossible to separate the focus on form provided by the materials from the fact that the experimental group was afforded increased opportunities for comprehension and use of the conditional. Further, the learners were better able to control the conditional in written than in oral measures. Finally, VanPatten and Cadierno (1993) report the results of a study comparing traditional, output-based instruction to input processing. The structure investigated was placement of the Spanish direct object pronoun. In the experimental group (input processing condition), second-year university students of Spanish were first presented with information about the placement of the direct object pronoun (object-verb or object-verb-subject, as compared to English subject-verb-object), and were then asked to interpret sentences using this structure. Results indicated that the processing group not only outperformed the production group on a sentence-interpretation task, but also performed as well on a production task. VanPatten and Cadierno conclude that instruction seems to be more beneficial when aimed at the perception and processing of input than when it focuses on practice as output.

QUESTION 6:   What can teachers learn from the research on grammar instruction?

Discussion

First, teachers can learn that the distance between any one study and their own classroom is large indeed. Although there is a great deal of evidence as to the benefits of form-focused instruction, especially in accelerating learning and perhaps in having an effect on eventual achievement, we have very little information on the how, the why, or even the who and the when. It is unlikely that all instruction will help all learners at all times in all areas and, quite probably, the mixed results reported here are due to our inability to tease out these specific factors. Further, because of the practical constraints under which real-world researchers work, we know very little about long-term effects of such instruction. It may well be that such effects (or lack thereof) will only show themselves long after the experiment has been conducted.

Second, teachers can also learn that grammar, as an instructional concept, goes far beyond the traditional structural textbook syllabus, to encompass areas such as semantics, discourse and pragmatics (Larsen-Freeman, 1991a, 1991b). Moreover, teaching grammar does not have to mean presenting a structure, practicing it, and then assuming that students should know it. Research in L2 acquisition, if nothing else, has shown that there is, more often than not, a lack of fit between what is taught and what is learned. Learners seem to have their own agenda and, to the extent that formal instruction fits in with this, it is likely to be beneficial. In the final analysis, however, teachers should always keep in mind the importance of their own reflected-upon experience. Language learning and language teaching are vastly complex activities that tend to resist the manipulations of researchers. Research, while providing insight and perhaps ideas, can never substitute for reasoned judgment grounded in a knowledge of local conditions—something only teachers can provide.

Bibliography

Bybee, J. L. 1991. "Natural Morphology: The Organization of Paradigms and Language Acquisition," in T. Huebner and C. A. Ferguson, eds., *Crosscurrents in Second Language Acquisition and Linguistic Theories.* Amsterdam: John Benjamins.

Carroll, S. and M. Swain. 1993. "Explicit and Implicit Negative Feedback: An Empirical Study of the Learning of Linguistic Generalizations." *Studies in Second Language Acquisition* 15: 357-86.

Chomsky, N. 1981. *Lectures on Government and Binding.* Dordrecht, Netherlands: Foris.

Clahsen, H. and P. Muysken. 1986. "The Availability of Universal Grammar to Adult and Child Learners: A Study of the Acquisition of German Word Order." *Second Language Research* 2: 93-119.

Cook, V. 1988. *Chomsky's Universal Grammar*. Oxford: Basil Blackwell.

Cook, V. 1994. "Universal Grammar and the Learning and Teaching of Second Languages," in T. Odlin, ed., *Perspectives on Pedagogical Grammar*. Cambridge: Cambridge University Press.

Day, E. M., and S. M. Shapson. 1991. "Integrating Formal and Functional Approaches to Language Teaching in French Immersion: An Experimental Study." *Language Learning* 41: 25-58.

DeKeyser, R. M. 1993. "The Effect of Error Correction on L2 Grammar Knowledge and Oral Proficiency." *Modern Language Journal* 77: 501-14.

Di Pietro, R. J. 1985. "The Place of Grammar," in R. A. Hall, Jr., ed., *The Eleventh LACUS Forum, 1984*. Columbia, SC: Hornbeam.

Di Vito, N. 1991. "Incorporating Native Speaker Norms in Second Language Materials." *Applied Linguistics* 12: 338-96.

Doughty, C. 1991. "Second Language Instruction Does Make a Difference: Evidence from an Empirical Study of SL Relativization." *Studies in Second Language Acquisition* 13: 431-69.

Ellis, R. 1990. *Instructed Second Language Acquisition: Learning in the Classroom*. Oxford: Basil Blackwell.

Ellis, R. 1993. "Talking Shop: Second Language Acquisition Research: How Does it Help Teachers?" *ELT Journal* 47: 3-11.

Eubank, L. and M. Beck. 1993. "Generative Research on Second-Language Acquisition," in A. Omaggio Hadley, ed. *Research in Language Learning: Principles, Processes, and Prospects*. Lincolnwood, IL: National Textbook.

Fotos, S. S. 1993. "Consciousness Raising and Noticing through Focus on Form: Grammar Task Performance Versus Formal Instruction." *Applied Linguistics* 14: 498-505.

Glisan, E. W., and V. Drescher. 1993. "Textbook Grammar: Does It Reflect Native Speaker Speech?" *Modern Language Journal* 77: 23-33.

Green, P. S., and K. Hecht. 1992. "Implicit and Explicit Grammar: An Empirical Study." *Applied Linguistics* 13: 168-84.

Hamilton, R. L. 1994. "Is Implicational Generalization Unidirectional and Maximal? Evidence from Relativization Instruction in a Second Language." *Language Learning* 44: 123-57.

Harley, B. 1989. "Functional Grammar in French Immersion: A Classroom Experiment." *Applied Linguistics* 10: 331-59.

Harley, B. 1993. "Instructional Strategies and SLA in Early French Immersion." *Studies in Second Language Acquisition* 15: 245-59.

Hatch, E. and A. Yoshitomi. 1993. "Cognitive Processes in Language Learning." in A. Omaggio Hadley, ed., *Research in Language Learning: Principles, Processes, and Prospects*. Lincolnwood, IL: National Textbook.

Heafford, M. 1993. "What is Grammar, Who is She?" *Language Learning Journal* 7: 55-58.

Heilenman, L. K. and J. L. McDonald. 1993. "Processing Strategies in L2 Learners of French: The Role of Transfer." *Language Learning* 43: 507-57.

Higgs, T. V. and R. Clifford. 1982. "The Push Toward Communication." in T. V. Higgs, ed., *Curriculum, Competence and the Foreign Language Teacher*. Lincolnwood, IL: National Textbook.

Ioup, G., E. Boustagui, M. El Tigi, and M. Moselle. 1994. "A Case Study of Successful Adult SLA in a Naturalistic Environment." *Studies in Second Language Acquisition* 16: 73-98.

Kelly, L. G. 1976. *25 Centuries of Language Teaching*. Rowley, MA: Newbury House.

Krashen, S.D. 1991. "The Input Hypothesis: An Update." in J. E. Alatis, ed., *Georgetown University Round Table on Languages and Linguistics*. Washington, DC: Georgetown University Press.

Krashen, S. D. and T. D. Terrell. 1983. *The Natural Approach*. Oxford: Pergamon.

Kumaravadivelu, B. 1994. "The Postmethod Condition: (E)merging Strategies for Second/Foreign Language Teaching." *TESOL Quarterly* 28: 27-48.

Larsen-Freeman, D. 1991a. "Linguistics and Language Pedagogy: The State of the Art," in J. E. Alatis, ed., *Georgetown University Round Table on Languages and Linguistics*. Washington, DC: Georgetown University Press.

Larsen-Freeman, D. 1991b. "Teaching Grammar," in M. Celce-Murcia, ed., *Teaching English as a Second or Foreign Language*, 2nd ed. New York: Newbury House.

Larsen-Freeman, D. 1989. "Pedagogical Description of Language: Grammar." *Annual Review of Applied Linguistics* 10: 187-95.

Larsen-Freeman, D. and M. H. Long. 1991. *An Introduction to Second Language Acquisition Research*. London: Longman.

Lightbown, P. M. 1985. "Great Expectations: Second-Language Acquisition Research and Classroom Teaching." *Applied Linguistics* 6: 173-89.

Long, M. H. 1988. "Instructed Interlanguage Development," in L. Beebe, ed., *Issues in Second Language Acquisition: Multiple Perspectives*. Rowley, MA: Newbury House.

MacWhinney, B. 1992. "The Competition Model and Foreign Language Learning," in M. L. Swartz and M. Yazdani, eds., *Intelligent Tutoring Systems for Foreign Language Learning*. Berlin: Springer-Verlag.

MacWhinney, B., J. Leinbach, R. Taraban, and J. McDonald. 1989. "Language Learning: Cues or Rules?" *Journal of Memory and Language* 28: 255-77.

Master, P. 1994. "The Effect of Systematic Instruction on Learning the English Article System," in T. Odlin, ed., *Perspectives on Pedagogical Grammar*. Cambridge: Cambridge University Press.

McDonald, J. L. and L. K. Heilenman. 1992. "Changes in Sentence Processing as Second Language Proficiency Increases," in R. J. Harris, ed., *Cognitive Processing in Bilinguals*. Amsterdam: Elsevier.

Odlin, T. 1994. "Conclusion," in T. Odlin, ed., *Perspectives on Pedagogical Grammar*. Cambridge: Cambridge University Press.

Pica, T. 1994. "Questions from the Language Classroom: Research Perspectives." *TESOL Quarterly* 28: 49-79.

Pienemann, M. 1984a. "Learnability and Syllabus Construction," in K. Hyltenstam and M. Pienemann, eds. *Modelling and Assessing Second Language Acquisition*. Clevedon, England: Multilingual Matters.

Pienemann, M. 1984b. "Psychological Constraints and the Teachability of Languages." *Studies in Second Language Acquisition* 6: 186-214.

Rutherford, W. 1987. *Second Language Grammar: Learning and Teaching*. London: Longman.

Rutherford, W. and M. Sharwood Smith, eds. 1988. *Grammar and Second Language Teaching*. New York: Newbury House.

Schwartz, B. D. 1993. "On Explicit and Negative Data Effecting and Affecting Competence and Linguistic Behavior." *Studies in Second Language Acquisition* 15: 147-64.

Scott, V. M. 1989. "An Empirical Study of Explicit and Implicit Teaching Strategies in French." *Modern Language Journal* 73: 14-22.

Scott, V. M. 1990. "Explicit and Implicit Grammar Teaching Strategies: New Empirical Data." *French Review* 63: 779-89.

Selinker, L. 1992. *Rediscovering Interlanguage*. London: Longman.

Sharwood Smith, M. 1993. "Input Enhancement in Instructed SLA." *Studies in Second Language Acquisition* 15: 165-79.

Sharwood Smith, M. 1990. "Consciousness-Raising and the Second Language Learner." *Applied Linguistics* 11: 159-68.

Sorace, A. 1993. "Incomplete vs. Divergent Representations of Unaccusativity in Non-native Grammars of Italian." *Second Language Research* 9: 22-47.

Spada, N. and P. M. Lightbown. 1993. "Instruction and the Development of Questions in L2 Classrooms." *Studies in Second Language Acquisition* 15: 205-24.

Tomasello, M. and C. Herron. 1989. "Feedback for Language Transfer Errors." *Studies in Second Language Acquisition* 11: 384-95.

Tomasello, M. and C. Herron. 1988. "Down the Garden Path: Inducing and Correcting Overgeneralization Errors in the Foreign Language Classroom." *Applied Psycholinguistics* 9: 237-46.

VanPatten, B. 1993a. "Explicit Instruction and Input Processing." *Studies in Second Language Acquisition* 15: 225-43.

VanPatten, B. 1993b. "Grammar Teaching for the Acquisition-Rich Classroom." *Foreign Language Annals* 26: 435-50.

VanPatten, B. 1992a. "Second-Language-Acquisition Research and Foreign Language Teaching, Part 1." *ADFL Bulletin* 23,2: 52-56.

VanPatten, B. 1992b "Second-language-Acquisition Research and Foreign Language Teaching, Part 2." *ADFL Bulletin* 23,3: 23-27.

VanPatten, B. 1988. "How Juries Get Hung: Problems with the Evidence for a Focus on Form in Teaching." *Language Learning* 38: 243-60.

VanPatten, B. and T. Cadierno. 1993. "Input Processing and Second Language Acquisition: A Role for Instruction." *Modern Language Journal* 77: 45-57.

Westney, P. 1994. "Rules and Pedagogical Grammars," in T. Odlin, ed., *Perspectives on Pedagogical Grammar*. Cambridge: Cambridge University Press.

White, L. 1989. *Universal Grammar and Second Language Acquisition*. Amsterdam: John Benjamins.

Yip, V. 1994. "Grammatical Consciousness-Raising and Learnability," in T. Odlin, ed., *Perspectives on Pedagogical Grammar*. Cambridge: Cambridge University Press.

Zobl, H. 1985. "Grammars in Search of Input and Intake," in S. Gass and C. Madden, eds., *Input in Second Language Acquisition*. Rowley, MA: Newbury House.

chapter 10

Vocabulary

Thomas C. Cooper

University of Georgia

QUESTION 1: With so many competing priorities, how important is it to spend classroom time on vocabulary learning?

Discussion

Learners recognize the importance of vocabulary acquisition as the most important key to successful contact with native speakers (Gorman, 1979), and they are open to effective ways of learning new words and expressions.

The importance of correct vocabulary usage is borne out by several studies on native speaker judgment of the severity of different types of errors commonly made by second language learners. [For a summary of these studies, see Ludwig, 1982.]

In one of these studies, Politzer (1978) compared six different error types against each other by having German native speakers indicate which errors in a series of paired sentences were the more distracting to them. The errors occurred in the areas of phonology, case endings, verb forms, gender of nouns, word order, and vocabulary. Errors in vocabulary resulted from confusion about word use (e.g., using the wrong word for "to know"), choosing a "false friend," and directly translating from English to German. In the majority of the native speaker judgments (77%), vocabulary errors were considered to be the most serious, perhaps because they caused the most difficulty in comprehension of the intended message. Politzer (1978) states, in summary, that "speakers of German seem to know quite intuitively that using the right words is the most important aspect of language use" (p. 258).

In addition to considerations in the area of native speaker reactions to incorrect production of words, there are other reasons for an increased emphasis on vocabulary learning in the classroom. When second language learners are engaged in speaking and writing, they can control the vocabulary load, by choosing the words and phrases that they can use with comfort and confidence. In contrast, in the processes of listening and reading, learners are dependent on the speaker or author. If they encounter words and expressions with which they are unfamiliar, they often fail to comprehend the message. [See Barnett, this volume, for a discussion of the role of vocabulary and vocabulary strategies in reading.]

QUESTION 2: How many words do students need to know?

Discussion

Estimates of the size and growth of native language vocabularies can shed light on the immensity of the task of acquiring a second language vocabulary. According to Nation (1990), research on the estimates of vocabulary size of native speakers of English suggests that freshman undergraduates use and comprehend about 20,000 words. When the learner is from one and a half years to 18 years old, vocabulary growth occurs at the rate of 1,000 to 2,000 words per year, or three to seven words per day. Estimates, however, vary greatly, and the figures quoted above would be conservative. High estimates indicate that college students understand 60,000 to 100,000 words (Mackey, 1965). Baumann and Kameenui (1991) discuss another interesting aspect of native language vocabulary knowledge. They point out that recent studies dealing with word frequency counts have shown that by the time high school students have reached their senior year, they will have encountered over 88,000 word families in their reading materials in school. (These word families represent about 180,000 semantically related words that have been reduced to 88,000 distinct word groups.) If the numbers are this high, the average student in grades 3-12 is learning around 3,000 new vocabulary items per year.

QUESTION 3: How can I help my students remember words?

Discussion

In order to expand their vocabularies, learners first need to employ effective strategies for committing new words to memory. Oxford (1990) presents some of the more effective types of memory strategies under four main headings: (1) **creating mental linkages**, (2) **applying images and sounds**, (3) **reviewing well**, and (4) **employing action**. Awareness of these strategy types, briefly summarized here, can aid classroom teachers in the construction of vocabulary learning tasks for their students. This section describes the memory strategy; sample vocabulary tasks that integrate these strategies are outlined in the next section.

1) **Creating mental linkages**. The goal of any cognitive strategy is to create mental linkages that will lead to long-term memory storage. The following are three types of strategies that focus on creating mental linkages:

   ♦ *Grouping.* These strategies involve "classifying or reclassifying what is heard or read into meaningful groups, thus reducing the number of unrelated elements" (Oxford, 1990: 58). For example, new words can be grouped according to parts of speech, topics, (e.g., farm animals), conceptual similarities (e.g., *hot, warm, fire*), etc.

   ♦ *Associating and Elaborating.* In this type of strategy, "new language information is related to concepts already in memory, or one piece of information is related to another to create associations in memory" (Oxford, 1990: 41). The associations must be meaningful to the learner, even though they may not make sense to someone else. Elaboration is the process of increasing the number of associations and connections by forming additional links in existing knowledge or by adding new knowledge (Eggen & Kauchak, 1994). For example, students can be given the word "money," and asked to list all the things they can do with it: spend, save, earn, make, borrow, loan, etc.

   ♦ *Placing New Words into a Context.* This strategy involves "placing a word or phrase in a meaningful sentence, conversation, or story in order to remember it" (Oxford, 1990: 41). The processes of association and elaboration are also used as the new information is linked with a context.

2) **Applying images and sounds**. A second category of strategies is composed of such tactics as the following: **using imagery, semantic mapping, using keywords**, and **representing sounds in memory**.

 ❧ *Using imagery*. The learner using this strategy relates "new language information to concepts in memory by means of meaningful visual imagery, either in the mind or in an actual drawing" (Oxford, 1990: 41). For example, a student could employ this strategy to learn the accusative-dative case prepositions of German by imagining a cat chasing a mouse through a house. This scenario could serve as the basis for a series of questions that would elicit accusative and dative case answers in a meaningful context: e.g., *Wohin läuft die Maus?* (*Sie läuft hinter* **das** *Sofa*.) and *Wo ist die Maus?* (*Sie ist hinter* **dem** *Sofa*.).

 ❧ *Semantic mapping*. This strategy depends on imagery for its effectiveness. Constructing a semantic map (sometimes the term semantic web is used) involves showing graphically how information is related and classified. This type of task serves to link the new to the known, or to prior knowledge, and to classify information hierarchically. It thus makes use of a variety of other memory strategies: grouping, imaging, associating, and elaborating.

 ❧ *Keyword*. The keyword method is a mnemonic technique for establishing an association between foreign language words and their translations. There are two stages to this approach. In the first stage, the learner thinks of an English word that sounds like the foreign word (or some part of the foreign word). This English word serves as the keyword, and it establishes an acoustic link between the two languages. In the second stage, the learner creates a mental image of the keyword "interacting with the English translation referent, thereby establishing an imagery link between the two words. So, for the Spanish-English pair, *pato—duck*, the acoustic keyword link is 'pot' and the imagery link is 'a duck sitting on a pot'" (Kasper, 1993: 245). Researchers point out that the more striking and unusual the image associated with the keyword, the more effective it is in calling to mind the meaning of the foreign word. [For discussion of research on the keyword method, see Ott et al., 1973; Pressley et al., 1987; Cohen, 1987; and Kasper, 1993.]

  Representing sounds in memory. New language information can also be remembered by using sound alone. The spelling rhyme "*I* before *E*, except after *C*" is an example of this strategy in English. Cognates are often easy to remember because they are similar in sound. For example, the German word for newspaper, *Zeitung*, sounds like "tidings," or *acqua* in Italian sounds like "aqueduct."

3) **Reviewing.** The sole memory strategy for reviewing is what Oxford calls structured reviewing or "spiraling." One exposure to new vocabulary items is not enough. If the aim is internalization, the learner needs to keep "spiraling back to what has already been learned at the same time he or she is learning new information" (Oxford, 1990: 42). Systematic reviewing also summarizes previous work and prepares a link between what has been learned and what is to be learned.

4) **Employing Action.** A final set of memory strategies deals with employing action, and includes are two specific strategies: using **physical response** and using **mechanical techniques.**

  Physical response. This strategy forms the basis for the teaching technique known as Total Physical Response, in which students listen to a series of commands and then act them out.

  Mechanical techniques. By mechanical techniques, Oxford (1990) means "using creative but tangible techniques that involve moving or changing something which is concrete, in order to remember new target language information" (p. 43). Examples of these kinds of activities are writing words on flash cards, sorting the cards according to some criterion, and writing contextualized sentences incorporating the new words. Combining the purely physical act of manipulating the cards with writing the new words facilitates the committing of the vocabulary to memory.

QUESTION 4:   **What types of classroom activities can help learners use these strategies?**

Discussion

  As teachers engage their students in vocabulary-learning activities, they need to keep in mind the distinction between **productive knowledge**, which involves the ability to use a word correctly in speech and writing, and **receptive knowledge**, which involves the ability to recognize and understand a word where it is encountered (Nation, 1990). Productive knowledge requires more from learners, since they must actively choose the appropriate word for the desired message. According to Crow (1986), some of the dimensions of productive knowledge are as follows.

Denotations and connotations. A learner, for example, should be able to understand the suggestive significance of "assassinate" versus "kill."

Syntactic constraints. Effective communication reflects knowledge of the grammatical rules governing the use of certain words. "Want" is followed by "to" plus an infinitive, for example, while "enjoy" requires the gerund form of the second verb.

Derivations. Productive knowledge of a word involves being able to derive verbs from nouns, to form the antonyms of adjectives, and so on.

Collocations. An important part of learning the meaning of a new word is learning what other words it goes with. While a "noise" can be "long" or "short," it can not be "tall." The verb "save" usually occurs with certain nouns, such as "money," "time," "souls," "energy," or "face," but does not occur with "secret," for example.

Register. Second language learners need to know which words and expressions to use in various social situations or contexts.

As has been mentioned, placing words in a meaningful context is an important aspect of vocabulary acquisition (Stahl & Fairbanks, 1986; Hague, 1987; Laufer, 1990; Nation, 1990; Spinelli & Siskin, 1992; and Omaggio-Hadley, 1993). Spinelli and Siskin stress the cultural dimension of context and cite an especially telling passage about the close connection between words and culture (1992):

> Every word, every expression we use has a cultural dimension. ... Speakers of a language share not only the vocabulary and structure of the language; they share the perceptions of reality represented by that vocabulary and structure. And because speakers of different languages have different perceptions of reality, no two languages show a one-to-one correspondence between vocabulary items or grammatical structures (p. 1).

Spinelli and Siskin (1992) present several activities for the Spanish and French classroom in which vocabulary is reinforced in its cultural matrix in addition to being reinforced in a situational context. For example, a classification exercise can be used to show how in French culture, beverage choice depends on mealtime: Coffee is never ordered with lunch, only after lunch. In another exercise, Spinelli and Siskin demonstrate how words for food items are rich in connotative meaning in a cultural context. For example, that which Americans associate with ham, the French associate with *gigot* (leg of lamb).

Omaggio Hadley (1993) stresses the semantic aspect of context. If new material can be related meaningfully to what the learner already knows, there is a better chance that it will be remembered more easily than information that is not related in any meaningful way to existing knowledge. To aid in meaningful learning, Ausubel (1968) recommends the use of **advance organizers**. An **advance organizer** is any device such as a visual, title, or graph that presents a structure for the new material and relates it to the learner's existing knowledge base. Semantic mapping and semantic feature analysis are two techniques for teaching vocabulary that make use of the principles of advance organizers. These types of tasks enable students "to visualize how new concepts fit into already existing knowledge structures" (Hague, 1987: 221). Hague outlines six steps to guide the teacher in creating a semantic map of a word:

1) The target word is written on the blackboard.
2) The class brainstorms words related to the topic.
3) The words are listed by categories in the form of a map.
4) As an optional step, students provide labels for each category.
5) Students discuss the words on the semantic map and, in so doing, discover how the words are related to each other.

Semantic mapping serves as an activity to introduce a word and then become a framework or scaffold on to which related words can be added as students expand their knowledge of vocabulary. In this way, learners come to realize that words do not exist in isolation, but are interrelated to other words through an intricate network of meanings.

Cross-cultural comparisons of semantic maps can also demonstrate for learners in graphic fashion the differences in connotative values and association networks that words carry within cultures.

For example, the German word for forest (*Wald*) varies greatly in meaning, depending on whether German students or Asian students construct the meaning network. In brief, while there are some common denominators, Asians find a forest to be a rather wild and hostile place filled with danger (*Gefahr*), wild animals (*wilde Tiere*), and snakes (*Schlangen*). Germans, however, perceive a forest to be a restful, quiet, and pleasant place (*angenehmer Ort*) where one takes leisurely Sunday walks (*wandern*), and picks mushrooms (*Pilze*) (Neuner, 1990).

Semantic feature analysis is another effective technique for helping students better understand the meanings of words by noting their similarities and differences. O'Donnell and Wood (1992, p. 142) note that "like semantic mapping, [semantic feature analysis] capitalizes on prior knowledge and demonstrates the relationships among concepts within categories." They outline three steps in the construction of a grid which lends visual impact to the activity.

1) The teacher chooses several words that belong to the same conceptual category. These are listed vertically down the left side of the grid. For example, the names of animals could be listed along the vertical axis.

2) Next, the teacher lists across the top of the grid some features that at least one of the animals possesses.

3) The grid is then filled in by discussing which features belong to each animal. Pluses (+) or minuses (-) are used to mark each feature.

"Clines" constitute another strategic learning activity that makes use of imagery in pulling to the fore the learner's prior knowledge of a topic in preparation for new learning. Clines consist of sloping lines (in-clines) on which vocabulary items are arranged to show degrees of variation. Nation (1990, p. 97) recommends that "the teacher [show] some of the points on the cline and then [give] the learners a list of words that have to be put in the next suitable place in relation to the given words and to each other."

In an example of a cline for adjectives denoting anger, the teacher could give students the following six words: *annoyed, mad, irate, furious, upset,* and *angry.* Then the students' tasks would be to rank these adjectives by degree of intensity on a sloping line with six rungs.

Research has shown that vocabulary learning is more effective if the teacher employs a variety of activities and does not rely on any one approach (Stahl & Fairbanks, 1986; and Baumann & Kameenui, 1991). Task variation gives the student "multidimensional exposures to a word to acquire different aspects of meaning" (Koda, 1989: 538). In addition, the different learning styles of students are better served when the teacher regularly uses more than one technique.

Ervin (1988) offers several suggestions for student-oriented, grouping, and classification activities using note cards. In one of these, students generate a list of animals whose foreign language names they do not know. The instructor translates the names and then gives two descriptions of each animal in the target language ("eats grass," "lives in trees," etc.) As a follow-up activity, each student is given four cards. Two cards contain the names of the new animals; the other two cards contain the descriptions. The students then go around the room and try to match names to descriptions. A similar activity is that of antonym matching. Each student has two cards and writes on each card one word of an antonym pair: for example, conservative—liberal; traditional—avant garde; peaceful—bellicose. The cards are redistributed, and students try to find the matches. In a final activity, which Ervin calls "Birds of a Feather," the teacher has written on cards foreign language words from three or more lists of categories. Some of the categories might include things you do outdoors, things you see at an airport, things that go bump in the night, etc. Cards are passed out at random, and students, working together, try to reconstruct the original categories.

These classifying activities could also be done without cards. Using their texts, students work with partners to find, for example, all of the words that refer to "things that are done outdoors," "things that are done alone," "things to do that don't require money," etc. It is important for the student to work with several different categories at once; when a word is associated with different categories, the multiple association involves repetition and helps commit the word to memory.

In general, we have to recognize that success in vocabulary acquisition depends to a large extent on the initiative and involvement of the individual student. In an article on fostering vocabulary development in the native language, Graves (1987) points out that "even if instruction in individual words were as widespread and rich as one could possibly make it, most of the words students learn, they must somehow learn independently" (p. 172). This statement applies even more to vocabulary learning in a second language, since the amount of classroom time in the foreign language is limited.

Graves (1987) recommends that the learner develop a personal approach to building vocabulary. Some suggestions are: keeping a file of novel words that are especially interesting; making an effort to learn a new word a day and then using it or trying it out on someone; using vocabulary building books; doing crossword puzzles; and regularly playing word games of various sorts. Helping students develop strategies and skills for self-learning may, in the final analysis, be the most important component of a vocabulary building program.

Bibliography

Ausubel, D. 1968. *Educational Psychology: A Cognitive View*. New York: Holt, Rinehart, & Winston.

Baumann, J. F. and E. J. Kameenui. 1991. "Research on Vocabulary Instruction: Ode to Voltaire," in J. Flood, J. M. Jensen, D. Lapp, and J. R. Squire, eds., *Handbook of Research on Teaching the English Language Arts*. New York: Macmillan.

Cohen, A. D. 1987. "The Use of Verbal and Imagery Mnemonics in Second-language Vocabulary Learning." *Studies in Second Language Acquisition* 9: 43-61.

Crow, J. T. 1986. "Receptive Vocabulary Acquisition for Reading Comprehension." *Modern Language Journal* 70: 242-50.

Eggen, P. and D. Kauchak. 1994. *Educational Psychology.* 2nd ed. New York: Macmillan.

Ervin, G. L. 1988. "Purposeful Practice with the Four-by-Six Card: Quick, Convenient, and Communicative." *Foreign Language Annals* 21: 337-39.

Gorman, T. P. 1979. "Teaching Reading at the Advanced Level," in M. Celce-Murcia and L. McIntosh, eds., *Teaching English as a Second or Foreign Language.* Rowley, MA: Newbury House.

Graves, M. F. 1987. "The Roles of Instruction in Featuring Vocabulary Development," in M. G. McKeown and M. E. Curtis, eds., *The Nature of Vocabulary Acquisition.* Hillsdale, NJ: Lawrence Erlbaum Associates.

Hague, S. A. 1987. "Vocabulary Instruction: What L2 Can Learn from L1." *Foreign Language Annals* 20: 217-25.

Kasper, L. F. 1993. "The Keyword Method and Foreign Language Vocabulary Learning: A Rationale for its Use." *Foreign Language Annals* 26: 244-51.

Koda, K. 1989. "The Effects of Transferred Vocabulary Knowledge on the Development of L2 Reading Proficiency." *Foreign Language Annals* 22: 529-40.

Krashen, S. 1989. "We Acquire Vocabulary and Spelling by Reading: Additional Evidence for the Input Hypothesis." *Modern Language Journal* 73: 440-64.

Krashen, S. 1982. *Principles and Practice in Second Language Acquisition.* New York: Pergamon.

Laufer, B. 1990. "Ease and Difficulty in Vocabulary Learning: Some Teaching Implications." *Foreign Language Annals* 23: 147-55.

Ludwig, J. 1982. "Native-Speaker Judgements of Second-Language Learners' Efforts at Communication: A Review." *Modern Language Journal* 66: 274-83.

Mackey, W. F. 1965. *Language Teaching Analysis.* London: Oxford University Press.

Nation, I. S. P. 1990. *Teaching and Learning Vocabulary.* New York: Newbury House.

Nation, I. S. P. 1982. "Beginning to Learn Foreign Vocabulary: A Review of the Research. *RELC Journal* 13: 14-36.

Neuner, G. 1990. "Mit dem Wortschatz arbeiten." *Fremdsprache Deutsch.* October 1990: 4-10.

O'Donnell, M. P. and M. Wood. 1992. *Becoming a Reader: A Developmental Approach to Reading Instruction.* Boston: Allyn and Bacon.

Omaggio Hadley, A. 1993. *Teaching Language in Context.* 2nd ed. Boston: Heinle and Heinle.

Ott, C. E., D. C. Butler, R. S. Blake, and J. P. Ball. 1973. "The Effect of Interactive-Image Elaboration on the Acquisition of Foreign Language Vocabulary." *Language Learning* 23: 197-206.

Oxford, R .L. 1990. *Language Learning Strategies.* New York: Newbury House

Politzer, R. L. 1978. "Errors of English Speakers of German as Perceived and Evaluated by German Natives." *Modern Language Journal* 62: 253-61.

Pressley, M., J. R. Levin, and M. A. McDaniel. 1987. "Remembering Versus Inferring What a Word Means: Mnemonic and Contextual Approaches," in M. G. McKeown and M. E. Curtis, eds., *The Nature of Vocabulary Acquisition.* Hillsdale, NJ: Lawrence Erlbaum Associates.

Rankin, P. T. 1962. "Listening Ability: Its Importance, Measurement, and Development." *Chicago Schools Journal* 12: 177-79.

Rivers, W. M., K. M. Dell'Orto, and V. J. Dell'Orto. 1975. *A Practical Guide to the Teaching of German.* New York: Oxford University Press.

Spinelli, E. and H. J. Siskin. 1992. "Selecting, Presenting and Practicing Vocabulary in a Culturally Authentic Context." *Foreign Language Annals* 25:305-15.

Stahl, S. A. and M. M. Fairbanks. 1986. "The Effects of Vocabulary Instruction: A Model-Based Meta-Analysis." *Review of Educational Research* 56: 72-110.

Thomas, M. H. and J. N. Dieter. 1987. "The Positive Effects of Writing Practice on Integration of Foreign Words in Memory." *Journal of Educational Psychology* 79: 249-53.

Tinkham, T. 1989. "Rote Learning, Attitudes, and Abilities: A Comparison of Japanese and American Students." *TESOL Quarterly* 23: 695-98.

chapter **11**

Testing

June K. Phillips
Weber State University

QUESTION 1: **Are there ways of testing students other than paper-and-pencil tests?**

Discussion

For over a decade now, second-language instruction in our schools has moved toward more "functional," "communicative," "proficiency-oriented" goals. These labels are similar in that they reflect concern for what learners can *do* with language rather than simply with what they know about its forms. Paper-and-pencil tests have traditionally consisted of items related to one another solely in terms of grammatical focus. The principal shortcomings of these tests were their inability to predict how students would perform communicatively in the second language in a real world situation where meaning and form must support one another in specific contexts.

Traditional achievement tests (standardized or classroom-based) provided numerical scores which enabled student ranking and grade assignment. These tests focused almost exclusively on written forms of grammar and assessed **mastery** of linguistic pieces, or the subsets of language, such as verb tenses, pronouns, and agreement. These discrete-item tests have not generally provided information on how well students convey **meaning** in a variety of realistic tasks. For example, a classroom test designed to measure the students' control over forms of the past tense, through a series of non-contextualized sentences, will merely require students to apply rules mechanically; it will reveal little information about the student's ability to narrate and describe past events in a real-life situation.

Testing practices should reflect changes in goals and approaches in order to inform students, their parents, and their teachers about the effectiveness of the language program. Today, second language acquisition theory (e.g., Canale and Swain, 1980; Ellis, 1985) characterizes learning as a non-linear developmental process. Current testing practice acknowledges the need to focus less on discrete language elements and more on **meaningful** use of the language in context and to address measurements of speaking, listening, reading, and writing as purposeful communicative behavior. To achieve this focus, effective classroom tests will not rely exclusively on paper-and-pencil tests, nor will they consist of unconnected items removed from communicative contexts. We shall look at specific examples in later discussions.

QUESTION 2: In our schools we hear about "alternative assessment." What does this mean for foreign languages?

Discussion

Teachers of most disciplines are finding that traditional tests inadequately measure more complex student abilities. Mitchell (1992) distinguishes assessment from testing, in that assessment carries the obligation to make a judgment. The kind of feedback provided by assessment enables us as teachers to say, "That communicates your thought but not quite precisely. Let's see how we might say it better." A form-focused test item will be marked right or wrong with no consideration given to the communicative value of the answer. Of course, better testing can also be part of assessment. Attempts are being made to make testing a more interactive process and to expand assessment into formats other than formal paper-and-pencil tests. For the most part, the value of "alternative assessments" lies in their capacity to tell students more about their progress over time. Many alternative assessments serve a diagnostic function as well, by permitting better "snapshots" of what students can do. Language ability, because it develops gradually, appears to be well suited to more open-ended and global assessments.

Shohamy (1991) advises teachers to use multiple assessment sources (i.e., tests, self assessment, diaries, projects, portfolio, observations, interviews, and peer assessment) for information. The teacher needs to obtain a variety of language samples that reflect goals and areas of emphasis of the course. A description of some of these alternative assessments would include:

  Portfolios. A collection of documents that provides evidence of the student's "performance." Portfolios can take several forms: "Best work portfolios" resemble those that art students assemble by selecting their best work in various categories. "Progress portfolios" contain samples of student performance collected over time on same or similar tasks. Portfolios are not limited to written samples; they can contain recorded or videotaped speech samples as well as journal entries in which students report or reflect upon listening and reading experiences. Several states have considered mandating portfolio assessment (e.g., Vermont, Connecticut, California), and software programs are under development to assist management and storage problems. [For discussion of portfolio creation and evaluation, see Tierney, Carter, and Desai, 1991; Mitchell, 1992.]

  Simulations. Short, contextualized role-plays built around real-world tasks are familiar to many foreign language teachers. They allow students to demonstrate their ability to sustain language in a realistic context and permit teachers to assess speaking.

  Interviews. Shohamy's idea of an interview is one in which the teacher seeks to obtain information about the language and the language experiences of the student. Through the interview, teachers might discover such things as whether the student reads in the target language outside class, or whether the student has found opportunities to use the language in the community (Shohamy, 1991).

  Observations. Teachers might want to assess how students use the language in cooperative learning situations or in small-group activities. The observations might suggest areas of need for later vocabulary presentation, for work on communication strategies, or for identifying the degree to which learners participate in group projects.

It must be recognized that relatively little research has yet been conducted on the effectiveness of alternative assessment on learning. Researchers are struggling with issues that go beyond the usual psychometric questions of statistical reliability and validity. Often the information sought from alternative assessment is for diagnostic or pragmatic purposes for which a number or score is of limited use. Consequently, some of the newer investigations in the area of testing concern questions such as setting performance standards for criterion-referenced testing, the role and procedures of self-evaluation, how to measure functional abilities, and the interaction of the learner with the context in which the test is taken. [See Henning, 1993, for a discussion of current assessment issues given new paradigms for language learning and testing.] What has been demonstrated is that grading criteria can be reliably applied by trained evaluators. Furthermore, observation and anecdotal evidence attest to the positive "washback" effect on instruction.

QUESTION 3: I am comfortable with achievement tests, but now we hear about proficiency tests and "prochievement" tests. What are the differences?

Discussion

As the profession shifted its focus to proficiency, or the degree to which learners can use language to pursue real-world tasks, it became important to create tests that paralleled these types of tasks. The task became the criterion, so that if one wished to see whether a student could maintain social conversation on familiar topics, one engaged the student directly in conversation on these topics. If one wished to assess the student's ability to get main ideas from a video broadcast on a contemporary topic, the student was asked to summarize what was heard on a televised report. Such real-world tasks are characteristic of proficiency tests.

The "prochievement" test grew out of classroom teachers' need for tests that were more directly focused on material taught in their program. Teachers also realized that the relationship between achievement scores and proficiency tests was imperfect. Many students could score well on achievement tests, yet, when faced with a communicative situation, they could not perform language tasks as teachers might have presumed. Thus, the desire for a hybrid test format arose (Omaggio, 1983) for which the term "prochievement" was later coined. In a "prochievement test" elements of achievement include: testing what was taught and administering tests at regular intervals. Elements of proficiency include: establishing a meaningful and realistic context and content, simulating real-life language use, challenging students to use language creatively to convey their own meanings.

Galloway's (1987) comparison of real-life challenges and classroom testing points out the differences that a hybrid type of testing hopes to bridge:

Classroom testing	Real-life challenges
meaningless, no context	meaningful context
other-created	often self-created
powerless, no control	active agent, control
expectations unknown	expectations known

impersonal	highly personal
unwilling involvement	willing involvement
unimportant	important
little knowledge gained	knowledge gained by self and others
extrinsic	intrinsic

(p. 51)

The key to good "prochievement tests," then, is bridging this gap. Phillips (1989) has suggested the following guidelines for classroom test development:

ℰ   Incorporate **tasks** and **purposes** into the test segments

ℰ   Provide a **meaningful context** for sets of items

ℰ   Include **global concepts**, not just discrete points of grammar or vocabulary

ℰ   Design items that allow **divergent** responses

ℰ   Allow the student to supply the **"sample"** of learned material

ℰ   Balance the test for **receptive** and **productive** skills

ℰ   Test the **objectives**, the **ends**, of your unit and not just the means

ℰ   Incorporate a **knowledge base** in support of skills

ℰ   Recognize that the test **recycles** language from previous units.

QUESTION 4: How can I test grammar in a communicative context?

Discussion

Many textbooks contain at least some exercises that are strongly communicative, even while focused on specific grammar points. Unfortunately, the testing packages all too often abandon the attention to function, context, and purpose that may have been built into the textbook exercises. After surveying a number of commercial test packages, Walz (1991) recommends that ". . . [textbook] authors should carefully examine the balance of achievement- and proficiency-oriented tasks, as many tests are deficient in the latter" (p. 182). Using guidelines such as those above (Phillips, 1989) or even the communicative exercises based on grammar in textbooks as a model, teachers may have to adapt or write these test portions themselves until acceptable published versions appear.

For example, teachers might need to ask the question: How does the grammar item under study manifest itself in real life use? If that question cannot be answered, one might need to readjust targeting the item as a major test focus! Let's look at adjectives in a beginning language class. Why does one use adjectives? Perhaps to enrich description? to render a story more interesting, more vivid? Instead of having students complete non-contextualized sentences or change forms to meet rules of agreement, teachers can devise a context that allows for meaningful, purposeful use of adjectives in natural situations:

Une description banale. Spice up this description a student wrote in French about an evening on the town. Do so by adding at least one adjective to each underlined word. **Attention:** Watch word order and agreement.

Nous partons à six personnes dans une voiture. Nous arrivons à un restaurant. Les serveurs qui y travaillent ont tous une moustache. A une table à côté, deux hommes bavardent. Ce sont le propriétaire et son fils. Un homme se plaint du restaurant à cause de ses chaises et son service. Lui et le propriétaire se disputent. Les clients quittent le restaurant. Nous, nous terminons cette soirée dans un bar où on a du Karaoke.

N.B. You may use adjectives from this list or substitute those of your choice.

ancien	dynamique	européen	excellent	français
gros	inconfortable	inefficace	jeune	mémorable
long	mécontent	noir	nouveau	petit

We're off, six of us in a car. We arrive at a restaurant. The waiters working there all have a mustache. At a side table, two men are chatting. They are the owner and his son. A man is complaining about the restaurant because of its chairs and its service. He and the owner argue. The customers leave the restaurant. As for us, we end this evening in a Karaoke bar! (Phillips, 1989, exam for FR 101)

old	dynamic	European	excellent	French
big/fat	uncomfortable	ineffectual	young	memorable
long	discontent	black	new	small

QUESTION 5:   How does one assess speaking in a large class?

Discussion

There is no easy answer to this question. However, speaking must be evaluated if it is a goal of the course and, today, most teachers and students value speaking as one of the most desired outcomes for the study of another language. The question posed addresses two aspects of testing, logistics and format, both of which are discussed here.

The classroom management question has not yet been subjected to research that indicates any one best way to accommodate all students in oral testing; rather, ideas on how to facilitate testing with large numbers of students have arisen from teachers themselves, who have experimented with various approaches. Rotation is one means used by many teachers, who do not attempt to test orally all 20-30 students on a given day or after a single unit. Instead, they may test three or four pairs of students on a role-play or in an interview. They do this during a written testing period, by eliminating one section of the written test (perhaps a writing sample) for those students targeted for oral assessment. Or, they conduct oral testing on a subsequent day while other students are assigned "seat work." The goal is to test each student once or twice during a term in an intensive (more than a sentence or two) format. Another avenue is through the use of audio and video recording of student performance, in the classroom or in the language laboratory. Again, this process may be done over a number of days. The secret is to plan meaningful activities for those not recording; that is, to engage other students in an individual or group project that involves them for the time needed to test. Pino (1989) provides useful advice for many of these management issues.

The format of speaking tests is a related issue. Simply taking time to interview students on discrete items is probably not worth the time. When time is set aside for speaking assessments, make it count by linking it to the contextualized, real world tasks that we want students to be able to perform. Adapted oral interviews that require use of recently learned material while allowing students the opportunity to express their own meaning can be spiraled throughout the grades. Many teachers follow Omaggio's (1983) suggestion and interview students in pairs. This approach cuts down on time, and students relax more with a friend at their side. When questions are not the "display" type (What color is your shirt?) and are targeted at an information gap (What did you buy at the mall, Tom? and you Judy?), the issue of copying or cheating does not arise.

In addition to interviews, oral tests might consist of role-plays, problems to be solved, video- or audio-taped messages, picture stimuli, and others. In essence, the teacher can turn any speaking activity into a testing situation, since the bottom line is to "test as one would teach." [For ideas, see Linder, 1977; Omaggio Hadley, 1993; Shrum and Glisan, 1994.]

QUESTION 6: How can listening comprehension be assessed without a lab?

Discussion

A language laboratory is useful for testing listening comprehension, but it is not critical. Most tests can be transferred to the classroom setting without affecting the process. If using a commercial test package where listening exercises are tape recorded, the teacher will want a good classroom player to compensate for the better sound achieved in a lab. Should that be impossible in a large classroom, one again might rotate students through the listening portion of a test by having them use earphones at a recorder in class or outside the room. Students with "Walkmans" might take turns listening at their desks, a procedure that allows students to replay the tape as often as needed if that is an acceptable condition of the test.

For teacher-constructed listening tasks, one might still wish to record in advance. This procedure not only ensures that each class hears the same message, but makes "make-up" tests easier. In schools with more than one teacher of the target language (or where an exchange student, parent, or other teacher fluent in the language is available), one might be able to record listening passages with more than one voice. Videotaped listening exercises or mini-dramas, especially when done by instructors, amuse students while testing their comprehension. Regardless of format, recordings should reflect speech at normal speed and with appropriate intonation so that students have a true feeling for the language in context.

Regardless of the delivery system, an effective listening comprehension test is linked to realistic tasks and provides for a "report back" device that fits the listening purpose and reinforces the realism of the task. The author and colleagues at the U.S. Air Force Academy created a number of "telephone message" listening tests at various instructional levels. Students responded by taking down in English on a photocopied message form, as much of the recorded message as they understood. They were also permitted to play back the tape as needed, since, in real life, this option would be available for recorded messages. Instructors also videotaped short scenes that related to themes studied, such as renting a car, ordering in a restaurant, advising about job-hunting. Students answered multiple-choice questions, gave opinions, and interpreted what they saw so that the test had open-ended components. The tests were all administered in the classroom.

QUESTION 7: What criteria should I use to grade open-ended speaking and writing tasks?

Discussion

Holistic scoring, in which the rater gives one grade as an overall impression of performance, has a long history in psychometric research and in foreign language testing. Educational Testing Service's Advanced Placement Test and its Test of Written English as a Second Language both utilize holistic scoring (Johnson, 1983). The Oral Proficiency Interview tester training program scores speech samples holistically as well. Reliability is the key issue in this type of scoring, and it is accomplished by training scorers to achieve an interrater reliability approaching a .85 correlation. This statistical measure means that the goal is set so that the speech or writing sample achieves a relatively consistent score by more than one person.

In the classroom, it is usually this same question of fairness that dominates our concern. In fact, the term "objective" is frequently used to refer to a discrete point test, while "subjective" applies to more open-ended formats. Perhaps we should begin to question what is "objective" about the decision to write an item on, for example, an irregular past participle. And is it really "subjective" when a panel of teachers agrees that an essay demonstrates high accomplishment? An important aspect of the scoring process for communicative tasks is the feedback it provides to students. Therefore, the teacher may want to score not only holistically but also analytically—that is, to provide information on subcomponents of the sample, such as grammatical accuracy, vocabulary usage, fluency or pronunciation in speaking, cohesiveness or clarity in writing. Or, scoring may be done solely on a global basis as measured against the task.

For example, a persuasive task of returning a CD to a store after having opened it can be scored on a scale from superior to minimal accomplishment. The teacher decides how many gradations to delineate on the continuum, including the option of pass/fail (task accomplished or not). Scoring writing and speech samples holistically requires that the teacher establish in advance a set of "rubrics" that describe various levels of accomplishment. Having a pattern in mind, one categorizes the student work at a level that best "fits" the product. With practice and the use of an "anchoring" sample (a paper that represents a category particularly well), one becomes consistent in grading. Groups of teachers can learn to grade one another's papers or speech samples reliably. One must be prepared, however, to communicate with students on how to improve their work. Omaggio (1983) has devised an analytic score sheet for student-paired oral tests. She grades students (A, B, C, D, E) with letters that carry numerical value (e.g., A = 5). Students' speaking is evaluated in weighted categories of

- ✎ pronunciation (x4)
- ✎ vocabulary (x7)
- ✎ grammar (x6)
- ✎ fluency (x3)

Weights are determined according to the teacher's emphasis. Letter scores in each category are tallied for a final grade determination. Somewhat unwieldy as described, the actual scoring sheet is less complex, and teachers gain facility in using it. While this system does provide students with feedback on their strengths and weakness within the language system, it lacks a "communicative" score. Pino (1989) has produced a more holistic score sheet for oral testing, and it, too, can be converted to grades. She uses a grid to evaluate students' speech in categories of communication, accuracy, fluency, vocabulary, and pronunciation. The grid places letter grades along the top (A+, A, B, C, D, F) with numbers below that reflect weights. For example, an A+ would render 40 points for communication, 20 for accuracy, 10 for fluency, 20 for vocabulary, and 10 for pronunciation; lesser grades carry decreased points, while retaining an emphasis on the communicative success of the speech sample.

Skills other than speaking can be scored holistically and with rubrics as well. Terry (1989) describes a number of communicative writing tasks and illustrates appropriate scoring procedures. Phillips and Bonner (1992) have developed a set of rubrics for assessing journal entries of advanced language students (see Appendix). The criteria are based on rubrics used in English classes, so that students are able to see similar goals established for first and second languages. The same rubrics may also be applied to writing samples on tests. Teachers, individually or as colleagues in a school, can design appropriate rubrics for their students. It is important that these criteria be shared with students in advance of the test.

QUESTION 8:   What are some ways of testing cultural proficiency?

Discussion

Cultural proficiency will have to be tested in different ways depending on the type of learning involved. If **knowledge about** the culture is the focus, tests of facts can be fairly straightforward: labeling rivers or cities, listing basic tenets of Islam when studying the Maghreb, describing reasons for the Spanish Civil War. If one wants students to be observant regarding cultural **behaviors**, the test might consist of a video segment in which students observe a scene, attempt to explain customs, or attempt to attribute behaviors either to individuals or society. If one wants students to **adopt** culturally appropriate behaviors, one might ask them to role-play and evaluate the degree of conformity to the culture their actions convey.

Since today's curriculum suggests that culture should not be an area set apart from language study, the testing of culture should go hand-in-hand with the testing of language. That is, contextualized testing of grammar, vocabulary, and the skills would be established on a cultural base. We are not yet seeing many examples of this approach. The state of Indiana has based its syllabus on culture and incorporates culture into assessment. An example of a Level III competence reported by LaBouve (1993) follows: The student plays the role of a tour guide at a famous museum. The generic cultural context is the fine arts, the specific cultural situation is the visual arts, the basic task is learned information, and the skills targeted are reading and speaking. Necessary grammar, vocabulary, and suggested evaluation schema are included in the testing guide. This type of cultural test will most probably be an area of future test development.

QUESTION 9:   What special testing techniques are most effective at the FLES (foreign language in the elementary school) level?

Discussion

Elementary-age students respond best to testing as they are taught (Curtain and Pesola, 1988). If the foreign language program emphasizes oral skills rather than reading or writing, then testing must follow this pattern. Many FLES programs concentrate on learning names for a variety of objects, with some conversation about self, school, and family. Testing procedures can combine listening with picture sequences, or mini-interviews can be conducted with small groups of children. An interactive story-telling might occur between the teacher and children in which children answer questions to carry the narrative along. Children can be asked to sort, to count, to choose favorite items from a box and talk about them. As in all communicative testing, the activity should be realistic and allow for divergence.

QUESTION 10:   What types of assessment can be easily modified to meet the needs of learning disabled students?

Discussion

A recent article by Sheppard (1993) advises foreign language teachers to work in tandem with specialists in learning disabilities as they design programs that address these special needs. Since disabilities take many forms, the foreign language teacher must discover successful learning strategies for individual students. Sheppard's work found that in the area of testing, many learning disabled students exhibited high anxiety when faced with an oral test. Teachers addressed this situation by not grading the first test, allowing for practice tests and quizzes, or giving unlimited time on tests. They used video extensively for listening comprehension, because attention was maintained with sight but not with sound alone. This is a very new student group for foreign language teachers, and we shall have to consult those with experience and expertise in order to learn more about them.

Bibliography

Canale, M. and M. Swain. 1980. "Theoretical Bases of Communicative Approaches to Language Teaching and Testing." *Applied Linguistics* 1: 1-47.

Curtain, H. and C. Pesola. 1988. *Languages and Children—Making the Match.* Reading, MA: Addison-Wesley.

Ellis, R. 1985. *Understanding Second Language Acquisition.* Oxford: Oxford University Press.

Galloway, V. 1987. "From Defining to Developing Proficiency: A Look at the Decisions," in H. Byrnes, ed., *Defining and Developing Proficiency: Guidelines, Implementations and   Concepts.* Lincolnwood, IL: National Textbook.

Henning, G. 1993. "Assessment Issues: Prominent Paradigms," in A. Omaggio Hadley, ed., *Research in Language Learning: Principles, Processes, and Prospects.* Lincolnwood, IL: National Textbook.

Johnson, L. W. 1983. *Grading the Advanced Placement Examination in French Language.* Princeton, NJ: Advanced Placement Examination of the College Board.

LaBouve R. 1993. "Proficiency as a Change Element in Curricula for World Languages in Elementary and Secondary Schools," in J. K. Phillips, ed., *Reflecting on Proficiency from the Classroom Perspective.* Lincolnwood, IL: National Textbook.

Linder, C., ed. 1977. *Oral Communication Testing: A Handbook for the Foreign Language Teacher.* Skokie, IL: National Textbook.

Mitchell, R. 1992. *Testing for Learning: How New Approaches to Evaluation Can Improve American Schools.* New York: Free Press.

Omaggio, A.C. 1983. *Proficiency-Oriented Classroom Testing.* Language in Education: Theory and Practice, Vol. 32. Washington, DC: Center for Applied Linguistics.

Omaggio Hadley, A. 1993. *Teaching Language in Context,* 2nd ed. Boston: Heinle and Heinle.

Phillips, J. K. 1989. "Prochievement—Towards a More Communicative Test." [Unpublished workshop materials.]

Phillips, J. K. and T. Bonner. 1992. "Guidelines for Evaluating Journals." [Unpublished classroom materials developed for the United States Air Force Academy.]

Pino, B. G. 1989. "Prochievement Testing of Speaking." *Foreign Language Annals* 22: 487-96.

Sheppard, M. 1993. "Proficiency as an Inclusive Orientation: Meeting the Challenge of Diversity," in J. K. Phillips, ed., *Reflecting on Proficiency from the Classroom Perspective.* Lincolnwood, IL: National Textbook.

Shohamy, E. 1991. "Connecting Testing and Learning in the Classroom and on the Program Level," in J. K. Phillips, ed., *Building Bridges and Making Connections.* South Burlington, VT: Northeast Conference.

Shrum, J. L. and E. W. Glisan. 1994. *Teacher's Handbook: Contextualized Language Instruction.* Boston: Heinle and Heinle.

Terry, R. M. 1989. "Teaching and Evaluating Writing as a Communicative Skill." *Foreign Language Annals* 22: 43-54.

Tierney, R. J., M. A. Carter, and L. E. Desai. 1991. *Portfolio Assessment in the Reading-Writing Classroom.* Norwood, MA: Christopher-Gordon.

Walz, J. 1991. "A Survey and Analysis of Tests Accompanying Elementary French Textbooks." *Assessing Foreign Language Proficiency of Undergraduates.* AAUSE Issues in Language Program Direction. Boston: Heinle and Heinle.

APPENDIX

Guidelines for Evaluating Student Journals

High Accomplishment   (45-50 points)
Fully reflective journal entry
Penetrating insight into the topic
Highly detailed response to the topic
High imaginative coherence in communicating thoughts
Considerable clarity in writing

Accomplishment   (40-44 points)
Reflective journal entry
Convincing insight into the topic
Detailed response to the topic
Imaginative coherence in communicating thoughts
Clarity in writing

Some Accomplishment   (35-39 points)
Some reflectiveness in the journal entry
Some insight into the topic
Some detail in response to the topic
Some coherence in communicating thoughts
Some clarity in writing

Lesser Accomplishment   (30-34 points)
Occasional reflectiveness in the journal entry
Occasional insight into the topic
Occasional detail in response to the topic
Occasional coherence in communicating thoughts
Occasional clarity in writing

Little or No Accomplishment   (29 or fewer points)
Little or no reflectiveness in the journal entry
Little or no insight into the topic
Little or no detail in response to the topic
Little or no coherence in communicating thoughts
Little or no clarity in writing